Prayers and Protection Magick to Destroy Witchcraft

Banish Curses, Negative Energy & Psychic
Attacks; Break Spells, Evil Soul Ties &
Covenants; Protect & Release Favors
Glinda Porter

Magickal Witches LLC

Contents

Introduction

Welcome to an entirely new realm of protection. In your modern world, there is a lot to worry about from the global-scale - climate change, political uncertainty - to the personal - a toxic ex, cyberbullying. Spell crafting can help you find comfort in a stressful world. This book will give you the tools to take charge and defend yourself mentally, physically, and spiritually.

The negative use of witchcraft, spell work, and psychic/energy work (collectively referred to as Black Magick) is a very real threat and has real-world consequences. These dark forces can be battled and defeated through the use of positive spell and energy work (referred to as White Magick). Within the chapters of this protection-focused spellbook you will discover how to banish bad energy; ward yourself against unpleasant/negative people; as well as defend your belongings; your spirit; and your space.

With over **50 spells and prayers** for protection, defense, and reversal magick; and a glossary of protective symbols, stones and other objects to keep on hand, this book will provide you with the weapons you need to cleanse your room and cast out old negative energies; put a protective and peace-preserving bubble around yourself as you ride the bus; deflect grumpiness and negative energy from people you work with - and so much more!

But negativity and curses are not overcome just with theory. It takes tangible positive action to address and undo tangible negative action. Through simple, understandable prayers and spells; through detailed explanations of the benefits of using magick to counteract magick; through lessons in how to correctly identify signs of witchcraft/psychic attack, you will be shielded and armed against Black Magick; you will hold the keys to destroying unholy agreements, and you will be versed in achieving and maintaining victory!

Magick has been hidden by its practitioners for hundreds of years, but now you can safely start your magickal journey **with information you won't find anywhere else**.

This book aims to be the shining light in the darkness - illuminating the path toward positivity, confidence, balance, and safety.

You may be thinking, "This sounds like some kind of Lord of the Rings, good versus evil, bull crap. Why would anyone hex or curse me?" We tend to believe that if we are good at heart and do not cause others harm, then everyone around us is doing the same. Unfortunately, that is not always the case. There are those, even in the seemingly supportive witch community, that perceive positivity and light as weakness and are all too ready to take advantage. There are also those who simply make mistakes and cast negativity accidentally. And finally, there are "dabblers" - people who may be temporarily angry or hurt and decide that reading a webpage on spell casting is enough research and end up putting something out into the universe which has far-reaching and terrible consequences for us. No matter the reasoning, the negativity placed on the unsuspecting recipient can range from annoying, to troubling, to devastating. We **need** to have an understanding of the ways to identify and destroy the negative effects that Black Magick can cause in our lives, whether it was intentionally or unintentionally placed.

Let me tell you about my first experience with negative, dark forces as a cautionary tale. In 1995, I was a wide-eyed, fledgling Wiccan. Wicca is a neo-pagan religion based on the worship of nature and universal forces. Not all Wiccans are witches, and not all witches are Wiccan. However, my intent was to practice spell work within the Wicca religion. Being new to the belief system and living in a rural setting, I did not have experienced Wiccans around me to provide guidance. Google did not even exist and the internet as a whole was still in its infancy. What I did have was access to a bookstore. So, I began to read everything I could to learn the ins and outs of the religion, as well as spell casting.

My third ritual ever was found in one of the many spellbooks I had acquired. It was presented as a spell to manifest an increase in light and happiness in the practitioner's life. I remember that there were many such spells, and I picked this particular spell simply because I already had the necessary ingredients. The spell included the casting of a protective circle, the common call upon the Goddess, and a few sentences which were described as calling upon a named Angel to deliver the "power of [its] light upon me". I followed the spell instructions and felt that it had been a successful casting session. Unfortunately, I was correct.

I had never heard of the Angel that the spell called upon. But, as I said, I was new, and I had no reason to think that any of the information in my prized books would be incorrect or dangerous. But that changed.

Within days of the ritual, I began to notice an increase in self-deprecating thoughts, along with a decrease in my natural confidence and sense of humor.

Within a month of the ritual, I had lost my job; withdrawn from friends; and fallen into a deep depression. Darkness had become a constant companion and hope was harder and harder to hold onto.

Within six months of the ritual, I found myself on the brink of total destruction. Nothing that I tried seemed to bring any joy. I was drinking at a very unhealthy level in an attempt to find relief from the constant weight of sadness. It was at this point that I was reading through a book on demonology I had just purchased. A passage in this book included, almost as an aside, a word that caught my eye. It was the name of the "Angel" which I had called upon in my ritual! For obvious reasons, I will not print the name here. Upon researching the being, I discovered that it was not the name of an Angel at all, but that of a Demon. My naivety and lack of research had led me to blindly call upon a Demon and request that it manifest its "light" in my life. That was the moment I realized just how powerful magick truly is. I have no idea whether the name of that Demon ended up in that book purposefully to cause pain, or if it had been a mistake by the author. But either way, the effect was the same. It nearly led me to become just another suicide statistic.

But the universe placed that demonology book in my path and, upon learning the truth and the cause of the train wreck my life had become, I immediately began to research how to reverse the ritual I had performed. The spell reversal I found was as simple as the original ritual had been. After gathering the ingredients, I performed the reversal and was immediately free of the oppression I had been under for so many months. My outlook on life brightened and my corner of the universe began to right itself.

And, yes of course, I have included that reversal spell within these pages! Not only did the experience highlight for me the power of magick, but also the need to be cautious in spell selection and casting; as well as the importance of understanding exactly what one is doing when performing a ritual.

This is not Harry Potter. Witches do not wave a stick, say some Latin words, and levitate people. Witches are manipulating powerful, universal forces to have real effects on their own (or other people's) lives. Those effects may benefit themselves or you, or they may be specifically designed to cause harm in your life. Once that threshold is passed and a witch is intentionally causing harm to another, the gloves need to come off. You can literally be fighting for your life.

You should know exactly how to protect yourself, your loved ones, and your property from astral attack. You should know exactly how to break a curse, a hex, evil soul ties, and unholy covenants. You should know how to be your own shield and your own sword. There may very well be no time to waste.

It is my solemn vow to you that after reading these pages you will:

- **Understand the practical basics and must-knows of protection and reversal;**

- **Have the skills and confidence to level prayers/incantations which will lead you into protection, growth, and more awareness of and deeper understanding of self;**

- **Know how to identify signs of negative energy work;**

and

- **Be able to destroy and reverse what needs to be destroyed and reversed.**

Evil and negativity are not concerned with whether you believe in it or not. Darkness will affect you equally whether you are just starting out in the Wicca religion, are an experienced practitioner of Wicca, do not ascribe to any particular religion, or are a devout follower of a completely unrelated belief system. The tips, explanations, energy work, and spells included in this book are not aimed to make you a Wiccan, or a witch, or a pagan, or a believer of anything. This book is designed for YOUR protection and to provide you with armor against evil, darkness, and negativity aimed at you from any source. And you can rest assured that every aspect of the spells and prayers included herein has been properly researched. No demon names here!

Quick Recommendation from the Magickal Witches team:

We would like to make the magickal journey you are about to embark on as smooth as possible. As with any journey, preparations need to be made, and there are tools fit for each witch, new or experienced.

In our case, we'd like to recommend the "Survival and Wellness Kit for Magickal Witches", which is completely free. Not using these tools is like making a trip to a rainforest and not taking any sort of tool to protect yourself from mosquitoes. You can do it, but the experience won't be quite as seamless as it could have been. It's discomfort that's not necessary and can be prevented. This analogy fits perfectly; if you don't have the right tools to go through with this process, it can be uncomfortable, and there is even a risk of not having a practice full of magick.

Besides, it's just an awesome free gift! Please, see for yourself. You won't regret it!

Scan the QR code to get inside the Magickal Witches toolkit for:

- 10 Elixirs For Detoxification and Aura Cleansing

- 12 Spell Jar Recipes For Protection

- Guide For Talisman Preparation For Use Outside Home

- 20 Daily Detox Tips To Keep Your Vessel Clear

- Master Ingredient Shopping List

It may not be completely clear why these components are essential quite yet, but in further chapters you will notice that this information will be very helpful. When you actually begin the practical side of the magickal work, you will come to understand. These tools are meant to alleviate some stress and obstacles that may show up along the way. For the time being, let's dive into understanding some theories that are meant to enhance the magickal journey you are here for.

Chapter 1
KNOWING & SIGNS

So everything bad, unwanted, and unfortunate that happens in our lives has a supernatural cause? Of course not. I can make all the poor decisions I want and then undo the effects through the use of the spells and prayers? Definitely not. To tell the difference between natural occurrences and supernatural effects we need to understand the signs of being cursed, hexed, or being under the influence of negative energy work.

Luck, both good and bad, plays a part in our lives, as does the perfectly natural circumstances of cause and effect. It can be difficult sometimes to identify the true cause(s) of events in our lives. For this reason, it is extremely important that we do not jump to conclusions regarding what happens in our lives. We gain nothing when we try to cause a positive change in ourselves by attacking from the wrong angle. We need to determine the true cause of our troubles and take the appropriate action to counteract or destroy those causes.

Upon completion of this Chapter, you will have learned:

- To define and differentiate between a "curse" and a "spell";

- To demonstrate a working knowledge of;

- Negative Soul Ties

- Covenants

- Agreements

- The dangers of practicing witchcraft;

- Psychic attacks;

- The types of witchcraft and curses;

- The signs of being under a witchcraft attack;

- The theory behind counteracting the power of witchcraft;

- The theory behind counteracting unholy agreements.

Here you will begin your journey into the world of fighting darkness with light, protecting that which is important to you, and no longer being a victim to dangerous, evil magick.

What is a "curse" and a "spell"?

A "curse" is defined as:

> "An appeal or prayer for evil or misfortune to befall someone or something." -The Free Dictionary

Honestly, that seems a bit too clinical to explain something so evil, fully encompassing, and broad. A curse can be placed on an object, an area, or a specific person. Its effect can be anything from loss of good fortune to death of multiple generations of family members.

As with most witchcraft, the intent of the witch casting the curse is crucial. One cannot "accidentally" cast a curse. Thankfully! The power of a curse does not come from the burning of a specific herb or the calling on a specific deity. The power of a curse is a reflection of the evil and harmful intent of the caster. To be successful in casting a curse upon an object, an area, or an individual, the caster must focus their rage, their dark desire, their destructive intent, every ounce of harm and hurt within them toward the goal of the curse. It is this wave of evil desire that the caster is sending out into the universe. Please understand that I am not being overly dramatic in my description. For most, the casting of a powerful curse is a very difficult undertaking because of the amount of focused intent required. It is not a matter of being momentarily hurt when you see your ex with a new lover. This requires serious, deep hatred. And luckily that kind of emotional output leaves a mark that links the curse with the caster - like when we touch any surface, we leave a fingerprint (a tiny bit of ourselves) behind on that surface, so it is the same with a caster and the curse they produce. It is this very link that will later help us to reverse the curse on the caster. But we have more to learn before we get to that po int.

A "spell", on the other hand, is defined as:

> "The means employed to effect some kind of change,
> to accomplish some magical action, to bewitch some-

one or something, to influence a particular course of
events or to inject magic into healing remedies or objects." - witchcraftandwitches.com

Spells are probably the best-known characteristic of witchcraft. They
can be positive or negative, meaning that a "curse" is actually a type of
"spell". A spell would usually involve the use of a protective circle, the
calling of a deity or some type of supernatural being, the use of specific
herbs or crystals, and an incantation or prayer.

Negative Soul Ties

Soul ties are created between two individuals through a powerful
shared experience, namely sex and/or marriage. That's right. We are
going to talk about the horizontal mambo.

Our modern society has taught us that sex is nothing more than a
base, carnal, physical act. But that is not actually accurate. Sex is much
more than that. It is a tridimensional experience - physical, mental,
and spiritual. When we give ourselves to another sexually (casual,
one-night stand or otherwise), we are actually forming a bond - a soul
tie - with that person. We are exchanging a bit of our body, our mind,
and our soul. Think about that for a moment. That means that, even
in a casual sexual encounter where we think we are just craving human
touch, we are deciding to give a part of ourselves to another human
and, in turn, receive a part of them to carry with us.

I immediately flash to the Nancy Reagan era slogan, "Each time you
sleep with someone, you also sleep with everyone they have ever slept
with." Sure, that was meant to be a warning against indiscriminate

promiscuity to avoid sexually transmitted diseases. But in a way, that slogan is correct on a number of different levels. In the same way that silly putty can pick up an image from a newsprint, so too does each soul pick up or transfer an imprint of itself upon the soul of a mate.

This is not some diatribe against sex! Far from it. However, it is an explanation and warning that our carnal actions do have universal consequences. Many people use sex as a temporary fix; a Band-Aid to cover an emotional wound. When the next morning comes and the "relationship" ends, a residue is left - like the glue that is left behind when you remove the Band-Aid. That residue can cause very negative effects in the lives of one or both of the participants. The effects can range from an unfilled longing to the scariest of all events in a one-night stand - the dreaded "catching of feelings". Humans are very distinct and complicated animals. Our limbic system is responsible for both the physical sexual response and the release of the chemical compounds that make us feel love. In that way, we are predisposed to link love and sex to a certain degree. My father implanted me with a quote that I have remembered and have seen proven true again and again throughout my life. That pearl of wisdom was, "Men give love for sex. Women give sex for love." Mind you, that was back in a time period when "man" and "woman" were the only two options, so an update may be necessary for today.

But what happens when you end up with a soul tie that keeps you from fully loving anyone else in the future? Or what if you end up with a soul tie who is not able to let go and move on with their life without you? Or what if you are married, and yet create a soul tie with someone other than your spouse? These would be examples of negative soul ties. They affect your life in negative ways.

Covenants

Covenants are spiritual contracts. They can be either positive or negative contracts, but for our purposes we will be focusing on the negative contracts. Who would want to destroy a positive contract anyway

Covenants are among the most difficult types of negativity to identify because the individual responsible for the covenant may well be dead and gone. A covenant with an evil entity can have effects lasting numerous generations past the maker of the deal. And the deal maker may not have even known that he/she was making a deal with evil. If you are familiar with the phrase, "a pact with the devil", an evil covenant is what is being referenced.

An evil covenant can be entered into by an individual on their own behalf or on the behalf of their child(ren). And the person making the covenant need not even have a full understanding of the terms of the contract, including the fact that the terms will result in destruction of future generations! Hey, nobody has ever claimed that the spiritual realm is fair, especially when dealing with evil forces.

As I explained in the introduction, as a new Wiccan, I myself accidentally entered into an evil covenant with a demon and was lucky enough to break the contract before the demon was able to succeed in taking my soul. It was a lack of attention to detail that very nearly cost me an eternity in Hell.

Like any contract, consideration must be received by both sides. So, the maker of the contract will receive whatever it is that they request, but the payment to the evil entity will ALWAYS far outweigh any worth the maker may receive. The only purpose of a covenant, and thus the only consideration acceptable, to evil is absolute and total devastation of as many lives as possible. Humans never, and I mean never, are able to come out ahead in a covenant with evil.

However, because it is possible for a covenant to be causing negative effects in our lives many generations removed from the maker of the pact, it is important to know how to battle and destroy the link between us and evil. Ways to disconnect from the destruction will be discussed in Chapter 2.

Agreements

Negative agreements can be grounds for a demonic attack against our lives. These types of agreements between two individuals may seem innocent, and even true, at the time but later are dismissed. Something as simple as "Will you marry me?" answered with "Yes, I will marry you." is an agreement. Perfectly sweet and innocent at the time. But what happens if the agreement ends up being broken and one side decides to not complete the agreement? Spirits do not forget.

One side or the other of the agreement may decide to dismiss the agreement. Both may forget about the agreement and just go on with their lives. But the spirits who witnessed the agreement and the joining through agreement of the two souls may not just let it go. The souls can use the breaking of the agreement to afflict one or both sides of the agreement until the agreement is properly resolved.

Although these agreements are made between two humans, they are witnessed by and held accountable to the spiritual realm. Your word truly is your bond. To break that agreement opens you to the possibility of demonic interference and attack in your life. Prayers for properly dissolving these agreements will be discussed in Chapter 2.

Psychic Attack

A psychic attack is an intentional attack by a witch to cause a change in an individual's luck, thought patterns, or emotions. It isn't necessarily a spell cast to cause harm (a curse) but could also include a love spell for instance. A love spell designed to manipulate one's emotions into loving another individual is a form of psychic attack. Another example of a psychic attack may be a spell designed to turn an individual's luck bad. Although a psychic attack is not specifically cast to cause "harm", it is a perfectly understandable possibility. For instance, a person may be deemed "lucky" if an air conditioner falls out of a 7th story window and narrowly misses them. However, if that individual's luck has been affected by a psychic attack, that same air conditioner may very well not miss.

The Dangers Of Witchcraft

Witchcraft is truly not for everyone, and it is certainly not for the faint of heart. It can be terrifically dangerous for both the witch and for their client or target. We must realize that we are dealing with forces that are far too large to "control". The caster is merely "directing" the forces. As soon as a witch becomes overconfident in their abilities and understanding, the universe and magic itself have a tendency to remind us just how human we are. In my opinion, albeit humble, there is no more spiritually dangerous activity than "dabbling" in magick. Witchcraft and magick demand our full commitment and respect.

A story from London, England, tells of a mother and daughter who became convinced that the 75-year-old woman who lived in the apartment next to their own was a witch. They also fully believed that a rash of recent bad luck and illness they had experienced had been directed at them by this woman. And so, they began to hold nightly, 9-hour, sessions of chanting toward the wall which separated the two apartments. The chants were loud enough to keep the elderly woman awake throughout the night and she was forced to sleep only during the day. The mother and daughter began to include more deadly and evil language, until they were heard chanting "Death by fire to the witch" for three straight nights. On the fourth day, the mother and daughter were discovered by a family friend. Both appeared to have burned to death in their beds, although there was no fire damage anywhere else in the apartment, nor even to the mattresses which the two women were found on. The story was relayed to British authorities by the old woman who was in no way found to be involved at all in witchcraft. The mother and daughter had misattributed their woes to a curse and had, in turn, actually become the very witches they were incanting to burn. Is this some antiquated, medieval story passed through generations as a fable? No. This incident took place in 2015

The above incident also goes to show that witch harassment is still alive and well in modern society. Witches may not be hanging in towns and villages, but the uneducated and knee-jerk reactions to the unknown still pose a big threat to witches today. These are the dangers that keep witchcraft secret and still only being practiced in the shadows.

There is also the danger of being swindled and scammed out of huge amounts of money. Fake faith healers, fake witchcraft supply stores, and fake clairvoyants are all big businesses. These unscrupulous scammers prey on the weak, the frightened, and the sad. Fake faith healers will take people for all they are worth with promises of miracle, supernatural cures. These scammers can be found across nearly every religion and in every corner of the globe, but are extremely prevalent in the holistic and charismatic Christian communities. With all of the evidence and information available to us with the click of a button, it surprises me that these sham "healers" still continue to be successful, but desperation can make otherwise rational people do some very irrational things.

Fake clairvoyants are of the same ilk as illegitimate faith healers, except clairvoyants are usually sought out by even more desperate individuals. Those who seek out easy-to-find, sham clairvoyants tend to have lost someone in their life and will believe almost anything that gives them some sense of peace. Through broad questions and reading of body language, a good scam artist can appear to have come into contact with some very accurate information. Not only that but they are well-practiced in keeping you coming back for more. With each session being worth up to $150-$200, even a fake can support a very comfortable lifestyle. Not to mention, some "clairvoyants" can even manipulate their clients into believing that a curse has been placed upon them that only the "clairvoyant" has the power to break...for a healthy fee of course.

And those are dangers if the witch is NOT legitimate. There are also dangers inherent in the practice of Black Magick. Any spell or ritual performed to cause harm to another person can, and often does, have repercussions on the casting witch as well. This is due to the Rule of Three. The religious tenet of the Rule of Three states that whatever energy a witch puts out into the universe, be it positive or negative, will be returned to that witch threefold. Witches casting black magick spells/curses, use a protective circle in the attempt to shield themselves from the effects of the Rule of Three. However, there are no guarantees when it comes to the Rule of Three. When we focus our intent on negativity, it leaves a stain behind; an indelible mark on the witch's soul that forever changes them and invites the Rule of Three.

Brief History of Witchcraft and Wicca

Although witchcraft and witches have been a presence since before the Middle Ages (references date back to the 13th century), the religion of Wicca is a relative newcomer to the world scene.

The "father" of modern Wicca is Gerald Gardner, although he never actually called his belief system "Wicca" because he preferred the more ancient term "Witchcraft". In 1920, Gardner was initiated into the New Forest Coven in Britain. It was Gardner's belief and claim that the New Forest Coven was a surviving group of original witch-cult members.

In 1946, Gardner feared that witchcraft was a dying and disappearing practice. So, he began his own coven, calling it the Bricket Wood Coven, with another former member of the New Forest Coven, Edith Woodford-Grimes. Gardner and Woodford-Grimes became the High Priest and High Priestess of the Bricket Wood Coven. Gardner implanted in his new tradition a lasting foundation of Wicca - the notion of an equal God and Goddess (this was terrifically unique and intriguing within the patriarchal, male-dominated society of 1940s Britain.) In this same year, Gardner initiated Alex Sanders into the Bricket Wood Coven. Sanders would later leave Bricket Wood Coven to form a new system of belief known as Alexandrian Wicca.

Woodford-Grimes only stayed with the Bricket Wood Coven for 6 years, citing concerns over the publicity that Gardner was attempting to bring to the religion. Prior to Gardnerian Witchcraft, all aspects of witchcraft were practiced in extreme privacy for the safety of the practitioners. Gardner, however, aimed to change the pact of secrecy of the religion and to gain popular understanding and acceptance. This proved to be a brilliant and well-timed strategy, but it did tend to make some traditionalists rather uneasy.

In 1953, Gardner initiated Doreen Valiente into the Bricket Wood Coven and she became the new High Priestess of the coven. With the assistance of Valiant, Gardner wrote the Bricket Wood Coven Book of Shadows. Many of the rituals in the Book of Shadows came from late Victorian-era occultism, but much of the spiritual content is derived from older pagan religions and includes both Hindu and Buddhist influences. Valiant was able to rewrite many of the spells and incantations into poetic verse. The partnership with Valiant was also short-lived, as she left the coven due to Gardner's continued publicity hunt and the new rules and restrictions which he began placing on the Bricket Wood Coven and the other covens following Gardnerian Witchcraft.

Gardnerian Witchcraft was brought to the United States in the 1960s by a British Airways employee named Raymond Buckland and his wife. The Bucklands were initiated into Witchcraft in Britain by Monique Wilson, a Gardner adherent. Upon their move to the United States, the Bucklands began the Long Island Coven. The Bucklands continued to lead the Long Island Coven until 1973, at which time the Bucklands stopped strictly following Gardnerian Witchcraft and formed a new tradition called Saex Wicca. Saex Wicca combined aspects of Gardnerian Witchcraft with Anglo-Saxon pagan iconography.

In 1971, American Zsuzsanna Budapest fused Wiccan practices with the burgeoning feminist ideals and politics to form Dianic Wicca. This tradition focused exclusively on the Goddess, Diana, and was completely made of female practitioners.

Although there are many different offshoots of Wicca and types of witchcraft, as we will soon see, Gardnerian Witchcraft was the first to step out of the shadows and show itself as a legitimate religious belief.

Types of Witchcraft

One could write an entire book filled with nothing but "types of witches". It seems that there are as many categories, sub-categories, and specializations as there are practitioners! But let's focus on 7 categories.

Folk Witch - A "traditional" or "Folk Witch" practices the magick of his or her ancestors, or of their general geographic region. The Folk Witch tends to take their magick as historical because it would have been practiced well prior to the formation of Wicca as a religion. The Folk Witch would most likely be a wealth of local information, having access to local availability of talismans, crystals, herbs, charms, and spells. Many Folk Witches have begun to blend the use of their "traditional" magick with more updated beliefs and modern tools.

Green Witch - The Green Witch focuses on their interaction with nature and the magic to be garnered daily from nature itself. A Green Witch is typically a rural witch and highly influenced by folk magic, with the center of their magical world being the home. The use of herbal remedies tends to be the specialty of most Green Witches and they often grow and harvest the herbs themselves, as opposed to purchasing herbs from vendors. Also, Green Witches are usually quite versed in aromatherapy using local herb blends.

Gardnerian Wiccans - Gardnerian Wiccans are one of only two forms of modern witchcraft that can trace its lineage back in an unbroken line to the very beginning of Wicca, i.e., Gerald Gardner. Although not all Wiccans are witches, Gardnerian Wicca is a British form of Wicca which is bound by oath to practice reasonable witchcraft. Gardnerian Wicca tends to be extremely practical with very little ceremony.

Alexandrian Wiccans - Alexandrian Wiccans are the second form of modern witchcraft able to trace its lineage back to those early days, i.e., Alex Sanders. Alex Sanders was one of Gerald Gardner's very first initiated into Wicca. Alexandrian Wicca is typically a blend of ceremonial and Gardnerian Wicca.

Eclectic Witch - Eclectic witchcraft is a catch-all term for witchcraft that doesn't specifically fit into any other category. The Eclectic Witch may be a blend of many different traditions, faiths, and folk practices. The Eclectic Witch can be thought of as the consummate do-it-yourselfer. They may take some traditional beliefs, some things read online, some things learned from a workshop they attended, and their own personal experiences; roll them all together, and come up with a practical method of witchcraft that works for them.

Ceremonial Witch - Ceremonial witchcraft, also called High witchcraft, uses very specific tools and incantations to call upon the deities and entities of the spirit world. Ceremonial witchcraft is a blend of ancient occult/pagan teachings. This type of witchcraft is held highly secret and many practitioners do not even identify with the word "witch" at all out of an abundance of caution.

Hereditary Witch - Hereditary witchcraft is a belief and practice system in which the knowledge is handed down from one generation to the next (mother to daughter; father to son). It is very unusual for any family outsider to be included in Hereditary witchcraft and it is just as unusual for the existence of such knowledge to even be discussed in the presence of an outsider, including sons-in-law or daughters-in-law. The relationship need not necessarily be a genetic one, as adopted children are seen as worthy candidates for Hereditary witchcraft. It is more a family tradition basis than a strictly biological tradition.

Angels for Prayer

Praying to angels for protection is quite literally as old as the first humans. More specifically, we are talking about archangels. An archangel is an angel of the highest rank. In Abrahamic religions, the archangels were created before any others and are seen as "leaders of angels" in their various tasks.

Angels are seen as the bringers of messages to humanity. Since the expulsion of Adam and Eve from the Garden of Eden, God does not come and speak with humans directly. Instead, angels are used as intermediaries. It was an archangel, and his angelic forces, who physically visited and ensured that Adam and Eve left the Garden; it was an archangel who visited Mary and informed her that she would be pregnant with Jesus.

However, archangels also have roles to fill directly assigned by God. Some are protectors, some are healers, etc. Not all angels are relevant to our topic of protection from evil and so we will focus on the relevant angels only. However, feel free to explore the others and add them into your prayers as you see fit. Just remember, from personal experience, you must research the names thoroughly and use pronunciation keys if necessary. Most demons were, after all, angels themselves before the fall of Beelzebub. And we certainly do not want to mistakenly call on a fallen angel to enter our lives.

The following are archangels named in the Bible and their assigned roles:

- **Gabriel**

Gabriel was the first angel created. The name "Gabriel" means "God is my strength".

Gabriel's ministry is promise and mercy. It was Gabriel who God sent to deliver the news of the coming of Jesus.

- **Michael**

Michael is listed as the Chief Prince of Heaven.

Michael's roles include: leading a host of angels in a victorious war over Beelzebub and protecting the angels during the end times. Also, Michael works to oppose Beelzebub in his rebellion against God and his attacks upon humanity.

Michael is a warrior and a champion. He can be called upon in times of battles against evil.

- **Raphael**

Raphael is among the highest-ranking archangels. The name "Raphael" means "God heals".

Raphael stands before the throne of God. Some of his duties include presenting the prayers of the saints and entering into the presence of the glory of God. It is also his work to heal the earth defiled by the fallen angels.

- **Uriel**

Uriel is an angel of wisdom. He is an archangel who watches over thunder and terror. In modern Christianity, Uriel is an angel of the divine presence, repentance, and archangel of salvation. Uriel means "God is my light."

Christians depict Uriel carrying a book or a papyrus scroll which represents wisdom.

- **Azrael**

Azrael holds the role of the angel of death. He does not cause death. Instead, he is responsible for helping the soul detach from the physical body after death and leading the soul to judgment.

- **Phanuel**

Phanuel is the throne bearer of God and the archangel of repentance. Phanuel is responsible for ministering truth and serves as the angel of judgment. Phanuel means "Face of God".

- **Zadkiel**

Zadkiel is the archangel of freedom, mercy, and benevolence. He also serves as the patron angel of all those that forgive. His influence on humans helps to inspire forgiveness to allow them to attain spiritual freedom. Zadkiel means "Grace of God".

- **Camael**

Camael is the archangel of strength, courage, and war. Camael is the leader of the forces that physically removed Adam and Eve from the Garden of Eden. Camel means "He who sees God".

- **Jeremiel**

Jeremiel has various roles, including assisting humans with clairvoyance and prophetic visions. He is also an angel of emotions and assists people to take a closer look at their lives. Also, he serves as the gatekeeper of heaven and watches over the holy deceased in their afterlife journey.

- **Ramiel**

Ramiel is the archangel of hope. He fills the roles of assisting with divine visions and guiding the faithful's souls into heaven. Ramiel, represents the mercy and eternal compassion of God. Ramiel means "God's thunder".

- **Ariel**

Ariel is the angel of nature. Her role is to oversee the healing and protection of animals and plants. Ariel also is charged with taking care of the earth's elements, including fire, wind, and water. Since she is a messenger, she punishes everyone that harms the creation of God. Ariel means "Lion of God".

- **Barachiel**

Barachiel is the patron angel of family and marriage. He is responsible for watching over converts to Christianity, referred to as God's adopted children, and helping them with their lives.

- **Haniel**

Haniel plays the role of divine communicator and acts as a direct passage between a human's lower energy and the higher energy states of the celestial realms.

- **Jehudiel**

Jehudiel is the angel of work. His role is to guide those in positions of responsibility by ensuring they work to glorify God.

- **Jophiel**

Jophiel is known as the angel of beauty and wisdom. She is the patron angel of artists and artistic illumination. She teaches the outer consciousness of Power of Light within oneself and sends fresh ideas to people.

Types of Curses

As with the types of witchcraft, there are MANY types of curses. However, given the fact that we are all living in a fast-paced technological world, there is less and less time available to perform curses that may take multiple days or weeks to complete. Therefore, instead of boring you with details on magick that is extremely rare, we will discuss 5 much more likely quick curse types. It is important to be aware and familiar with the types of curses when it comes to successfully spotting the signs of being cursed!

Spitting Curses - Yep. The least hygienic way to possibly curse someone. The most effective spitting curses are performed by actually spitting directly on the target. But, thankfully, that is pretty tricky to get away with in modernity... and definitely in the age of Covid-19! However, these curses can also be performed by spitting in front of or behind the person with the proper intent. Or even on something the target is likely to touch, like a door handle or keyboard. If you are a germaphobe, I apologize for putting these images in your head, but knowledge is power. Moving on!

The Evil Eye - It may sound like some kind of punchline to a Golden Girls episode, but it is all too real. The evil eye is a large output of evil intent directed while staring at the target of the curse. Because we have learned that intent released into the universe is really the backbone to all spells and curses, this should make sense. Gathering all of the evil, wicked intent and imagery the witch can muster and releasing it all at once toward a target he or she is in visual contact with is actually quite a powerful and dangerous weapon.

Verbal Curses - Pretty self-explanatory probably. These are short incantations that can be repeated over and over while releasing the evil intent of the curse into the universe. It is frightening just how simple it is to find ready-made verbal curses with just a quick Google search, not to mention that some of the most powerful and appropriately directed verbal curses actually spring from the creativity of the casting witch!

Written Curses - With written curses, the casting witch can write the evil intent on a slip of paper and conceal the paper on or near the target. Written curses are actually quite powerful, especially if combined with an accompanying verbal curse to add to the destruction.

Object Curses - Object curses are probably the most common type and, unfortunately, also the most long-lasting. An object curse is not directed at a specific person but is instead placed on an inanimate object. This allows the curse to affect anyone and everyone who comes into contact with the object. That's right folks. We are talking about the kind of curse that was attached to the lava rock in The Brady Bunch - Hawaii episode! And if you don't know what I am talking about, are you sure you are old enough to be reading this book?!

There are two big issues when it comes to object curses. First, they may have been unintentionally cursed. If the object was very near or extremely special to an individual who exuded or was a victim of rampant, sustained evil, the object may have picked up the evil by transference. Murder weapons used for bludgeoning or cutting a victim to death are notorious for becoming "cursed objects". Not because they were cursed by a witch, but because of the evil which was poured out through them.

The second issue is that the object may not be "cursed" at all but may instead be haunted. Many times, this is the case with "cursed" dolls. Instead of having a curse placed on them, dolls are actually ripe vessels for demons or evil souls to inhabit. Real examples of haunted dolls with "cursed" histories include "Annabelle" held by the Estate of Ed and Lorraine Warren; "Robert The Doll" exhibited by the East Martello Museum in Key West, Florida; and "Harold The Doll" held by Zack Baggins in Las Vegas, NV. Removing a "curse" from a haunted object will have no effect whatsoever, except perhaps to anger the already demented spirit within.

Reading the Signs - **How to know if you are under a witchcraft attack**

First and foremost, witchcraft or psychic attack should not be among the first things you assume is wrong with you! If you are having physical symptoms, go to your doctor. If you are having psychological symptoms, go to your therapist. It is absolutely imperative that you rule out natural, logical causes before moving on to otherworldly, supernatural ones. Usually, there is a perfectly legitimate and understandable medical or psychological reason for what is happening.

The keyword in that sentence is "usually". Let's assume that you have ruled out any cause for your distress here on this plane. What next? Well, it is time to take a look at your life for signs of a psychic attack through witchcraft.

Signs that you are under attack can vary wildly based on the type of curse, the intended result, and the knowledge of the caster. For instance, a curse designed to cause you depression and increase your self-loathing will have different signs than a curse designed to cause physical damage to your heart. There are, however, some general signs which are common to all curses. These are the signs we will be taking a look at.

Planting the Seed - Curses, and magick in general, become more powerful when the target is aware of the intent. So, if the caster is determined to cause the desired effect in your life, they may very well tell you about the curse. Or, if they have an outwardly positive relationship with you, they may merely hint at the possibility of a curse just to plant the seed of thought in your mind. If someone tells you that they have cursed you, it's safest to believe it and act accordingly.

Unexplainable Physical Sickness - If you develop some kind of physical ailment that your doctor is unable to explain and control with modern medicine, someone may be attacking you. Headaches/migraines are a common physical symptom of psychic attack. But remember, we only get to this point by ruling out the more probable medical reasons. It is also common for a new and unexplainable hormonal imbalance to arise. This is because the pineal gland (otherwise known as the Third Eye) in the brain is responsible for hormone regulation. If our Third Eye is sensing an ongoing psychic attack, our hormonal balance can be greatly affected.

Lethargy and/or Inability to Sleep - Although it just sounds like a normal day of Covid quarantine, blobbing out on the couch and not being able to form much desire to do anything is actually a sign of psychic attack. That type of extreme lethargy can be coupled with the inability to actually get restorative sleep. If these symptoms are a result of a psychic attack, the purpose may be to destroy your quality of life, affect your physical and mental health, or even cause you to lose your job. However, these are also symptoms of depression, which highlights the importance of seeking medical guidance first.

Nightmares - As our conscious mind rests, our subconscious mind processes and plays out the inner dialogue of the psyche. When our guard is down and we are not able to consciously process or control our experience, curses can be very active. Now, not every occasional nightmare is a sign of a psychic attack. The nightmares we are talking about here are persistent and recurring. If you are having the same type of nightmare repeatedly, nightly, you may be experiencing a psychic attack.

Depression/Oppression without cause - Despite adequate nutrition, counseling, and medication, something just keeps weighing you down. This odd feeling of being unsettled can be an indication of the presence of negative energy or an evil attachment.

Paranoia - This type of mental effect usually manifests as a feeling of being watched, or a feeling that your thoughts and the thoughts of those around you are being invaded or monitored by someone else. These feelings can, and are actually designed to, convince you and those around you that you are going insane and cannot be fully trusted. It is a truly surreal situation to be in when you no longer are sure you can trust your own senses, your own inner dialogue. Again, paranoid delusions are a well-known psychological disorder so make sure to rule out any such pedantic explanation first.

Patterns and Symbols - These are the types of things we tend to think about as signs or omens. These can take an endless number of forms, but the most important part is that they will be most apparent to the target. Our Third Eye can filter mere coincidence from true patterns and symbology. For example, if you wake up on your own at 4:18 a.m. every morning for a week and look at the clock, your pineal gland will discern whether it just happened that way or if it is a sign. Follow your instincts when it comes to patterns and/or signs. Go with your gut.

Loss of Time and Memory - You may experience gaps in your memory where you cannot account for the amount of time that has passed. This occurs as your worldly outlook begins to steadily turn inward. Time becomes irrelevant because you are dealing with so many other, seemingly more pressing, issues. You may have no memory of meeting people, going to places, or the things you have done during these periods. It is as if you exist on a separate timeline from those around you and can lead to some very disturbing and awkward situations.

Animals acting oddly in your presence - Animals are far more emotionally intelligent than we commonly give them credit for. There is a reason that animals have been used as "familiars" by witches stretching back into antiquity. They have a very strong connection to the spirit world and are able to sense when something is not quite right. A change in an animal's behavior when they are around you may signal that you are under attack from the spirit world.

Destroying the Power of Witchcraft & Unholy Agreements

Now that we have discussed definitions, types, dangers, and signs of witchcraft interference in our lives, it is time to begin arming ourselves against attack. No one deserves the terrible consequences that can arise from a psychic attack. The negativity - the evil born into the universe as a result of a curse - is an abomination and an affront to the purity and light of the universe.

Agreements made with dark and evil forces, demons, whatever you wish to call them is equally as destructive and unnatural as a curse. Holding true to an oath and following through with one's word should not be an exception, but the accepted rule in all things. As such, a broken agreement that invites darkness and evil into the equation must be properly undone.

The power to fight against and destroy these forces within our lives, along with the devastation and soul-crushing darkness they bring, resides in each of us. What vanquishes darkness? Light. What has the power to sever the chord holding us hostage to the whims of a curse-casting witch? Prayer and Incantation. Through the power of releasing light (good intentions) into the universe by way of prayer or incantation, we hold the ability to end psychic attacks against us. And through the power of releasing good intentions into the universe via prayer or incantation, we have the ability to successfully break agreements that have invited evil into our lives.

Chapter 2
PRAYERS &
PROTECTION
SPELLS

Throughout this book, it has been my intention to completely avoid discussing religion. However, we are now in a section where it is going to be pretty much impossible to ignore it. Please understand that the power of the prayers and spells in this chapter do not come from the language used, but from the focused intent of the person reciting the prayer. If you find a prayer that resonates with you but contains the name of a deity to which you have no connection, there is no reason you cannot substitute a deity from your personal belief in its place. Or even simply use the term "universe".

With that being said, I will attempt to provide prayers and spells directly from as many religious backgrounds as possible. Read through each section and find those prayers or spells which speak to you and your experience.

As a specific note to my Christian brethren, I implore you not to skip over the "spells" in this chapter. While it is true that the faiths of Christianity and Wicca/Paganism/Occultism have been at odds for...well...more than 2,000 years now, demons and evil do not care if you believe in it or not. Quite frankly, a strong Christian faith actually puts you in more danger of a psychic attack from evil forces because Satan would most assuredly enjoy watching a saved soul squirm. In other words, just as Jesus worked in the supernatural realm, or should I say he came from the supernatural realm, you must be willing to fight for your health, safety, and well-being wherever it is being challenged.

The powers of evil and personal destruction that accompany a curse, a negative soul tie, an unholy covenant, or a broken agreement can be extremely strong and grow like a tumor, embedding themselves deep in our lives and psyche. It may, and most likely will, take more than one prayer or spell to free ourselves from this type of darkness.

This is not a one-and-done situation. I visualize curses and the other types of psychic attacks much like a mangrove tree. What appears on the surface to be a large swath of mangrove trees of many acres, or even an entire swamp, can actually be only one large mangrove tree. As the roots of a mangrove grow, they spread in all directions, not just down into the earth, and produce periodic shoots back above the surface. These become what appear to be separate and distinct trees but are actually part of the original root system.

So, it is the same with curses and darkness in our lives. What might appear to be unconnected traits or instances of negativity may, in fact, all be fed by the same curse. Just as you would not expect to kill a 4-acre wide mangrove system by chopping down one of the trees on the surface, we cannot expect to break a widespread curse that has pervaded many aspects of our lives by saying a prayer once and then moving on.

That is why we need to see the fight against darkness as an ongoing war and not just a single battle. We need to be willing to fight for ourselves, our destiny, and our bloodline. It may take repeating the same prayer once per day, or once per week, over an extended period of time to finally dig out the last effects of a curse in our lives. It may take performing the same ritual on successive new moons for a number of months to break a strong curse. It may even take a combination of the two! But please know that we are on the side of good, of light, of love, and of righteousness. We WILL prevail.

When you should utilize these prayers is completely up to you and your needs. The line of prayer is always open. That is the beautiful thing about prayer, it takes very little preparation and there is never a bad time to pray. It is important to focus and calm your spirit, open your heart and mind, and pray. Pray with all your heart. Pray often. And pray hard.

Utilizing these spells and rituals is slightly different. Spell work is normally performed at night, under the light of the moon. Unless otherwise noted within the spell, it is safe to assume that the spells and rituals are meant to be performed at the time of the waxing moon. Also, there is a specific way to maximize the power you are putting out into the universe - try to perform your ritual near running water (i.e., a creek, a river, an underground spring, etc.). The electromagnetic energy created by running water is a natural, measurable fact. It is electromagnetic energy that powers our intentions into the universe and into the spiritual plane. Therefore, if you are able to be near a source of electromagnetic energy, your intention will gain strength merely by being in the location. As you are preparing yourself for the ritual, focus your intention and calm your spirit, cast your protective circle, and make your intentions known.

How can we tell if our prayers and rituals are actually working? Well, have you ever tried to organize and clean out a garage? I always end up with boxes and piles of stuff sitting all over the driveway and yard at first. It pretty much becomes just a mass of controlled chaos because there is so much to unpack and go through to make sense of it all. It actually gets worse before it gets better. But then, the useful items get matched together, while the items which have gone bad or are no longer necessary are discarded. Order starts to form out of the chaos and, slowly but surely, everything starts to fall back into place nicely.

That is essentially how the breaking of psychic attacks and removal of evil from our lives will work as well. At first, things may seem to get worse. It may seem counterintuitive, but that means you are doing something right. Satan, evil, darkness - whatever you choose to call it - does not give up and release power easily or willingly. As you begin your work to rid yourself of negativity, darkness will double down. STAY STRONG. STAY THE COURSE. Positivity and light will begin to reign in your life. Order will begin to form out of the internal chaos and a feeling of peace and freedom from oppression will fall back into its rightful spot within you.

Cleansing and maintaining victory will be discussed in Chapter 3. Do not believe that once you have broken a curse or negative soul tie, you are free and clear. There will still be work to be done.

The Right to Reverse A Curse

In the following pages, you will find prayers and spells to break curses, and prayers and spells to reverse curses, negativity, and evil. To "reverse" a curse means to send the negativity back to the individual who placed the curse on you. You can think of reversal as sliding a mirror in between you and whoever placed the curse. The negativity reflects off of the mirror and shoots back in the other person's direction. Reversal is a wonderful option to rid yourself of negativity and to do so in accordance with universal laws. These universal laws include the concept of "like attracts like" and The Rule of Three.

In case you feel that you should never reverse black magick, let's discuss a bit about how the spiritual plane functions. On the spiritual plane, like attracts like. This means that it is not unusual to find negative energy zipping back and forth. When an individual performs a ritual or places a curse on you, your family, or your belongings, they are quite aware that the concept of "like attracts like" means that performing black magick opens one up to darkness. The focus and evil intent that it takes to saddle another individual with a curse announces to the universe that this person is open to negativity. Just as we can manifest good and light in our lives through focus and visualization, black magick uses the same concept to manifest evil and darkness in their life through their actions.

Further, any witch who is powerful and versed enough to successfully place a curse will also be aware of the Wiccan Rede (aka Rule of Three). A "Rede" is not something that a Wiccan or witch repeats as part of a spell or incantation, it is more of a guiding principle, or advice passed on from an adherent to a new follower. The Wiccan or witchcraft Rede states:

"Bide the Wiccan Law ye must,

In perfect love and perfect trust.

Eight words the Wiccan Rede fulfill:

If ye harm none, do what ye will.

What ye send forth comes back to thee

So ever mind the Law of Three.

Follow this with mind and heart,

Merry ye meet, and merry ye part."

The Wiccan Rede decrees that whatever type of energy one puts out into the universe will be returned to them threefold, be it positive or negative. The Rede stands as a warning against the use of black magick to avoid the threefold return of evil into their lives. However, humans tend to be greedy and spiteful creatures. And so, against all advice and against the Rede, humans will continue to flaunt the rules at every opportunity. Their insolence will lead to the return of their own punishment threefold.

For these reasons, there is no need to feel hesitant about reversing black magick onto its practitioner. It is completely natural and within the universal laws to do so. Because "like attracts like" the energy or evil will find its way back to the castor. The castor, the person who casts the curse, quite literally manifests or creates evil and darkness in order to mold it into the curse they want, it does not exist on its own or in a vacuum. Every curse needs a castor to come into being. This is why there is an undeniable and unearthly link between a curse and its castor. It is not wrong, evil, dangerous, or even shocking to return a creation to its creator. When we reverse a curse or evil intention placed on us, that is what we are doing - returning it to its creator (in threefold fo rm).

Now, finally, let's grab our armor and sword and step into the fight.

Prayers To Destroy The Power of Witchcraft

#1

I thank you, God (or Goddess, Universe, Angels, Spirit, Ascended Masters, Protectors, etc.), for giving me authority and power to defeat the kingdom of darkness. I thank you for the authority that I have in you to overcome and defeat witchcraft, Jezebel, and their father the devil.

Through our Lord (or Goddess, Universe, Angels, Spirit, Ascended Masters, Protectors, etc.), you have given me authority to trample on snakes and scorpions and to overcome all the power of the enemy and nothing will harm me.

You have decreed that whatever I bind on earth will be bound in heaven, and whatever I release on the earth will be released in heaven, and that if two of us on the earth agree about anything we ask for, it will be done for us exactly as we agreed.

Amen and Blessed Be.

#2

My Lord (or Goddess, Universe, Angels, Spirit, Ascended Masters, Protectors, etc.), I have authority and power over the spirits of witchcraft, Jezebel, wickedness and disfavor. I have power over the decisions and activities of the powers of darkness at all levels. As I stand in this divine agreement and pray this day, I will accept my victory over witchcraft and the works of darkness in my life and in my family.

I reject every form of authority of the devil and of authority of the witchcraft world over my life and family.

Let the walls and defenses of evil witchcraft against my life, my destiny and my family be torn down. Frustrate every witch; every wizard; every Jezebel against my life and my family.

I break the power of witchcraft's deception, seduction, sorcery, domination and intimidation over my life and my family. I command every evil seed in the form of strife, quarrels, disfavor, hatred, nightmares, illnesses, and confusions planted in my life or in my family be uprooted by fire this moment.

Amen and Blessed Be.

#3

I hold myself as a being of light. I declare myself to be kept free of the captive and limiting power of darkness. I do hereby rebuke the use of all malicious and harmful magick for any purposes. Let not what I rebuke be used upon or against me; my family; my destiny; or my possessions.

The balance of nature shall be found elsewhere other than within the pure splendor and blessings of the light which shines from and upon me.

Allow my goodness to prevail against any evil settling upon me either in my past, present or future.

Amen and Blessed Be.

#4

Lord (or Goddess, Universe, Angels, Spirit, Ascended Masters, Protectors, etc.) I ask that you forgive me in any way I have surrendered myself to men or women who come in your name but are using evil powers. I believe that I did not listen enough to you, which was why I submitted to their tricks. I believe you tried to warn me, but perhaps I placed my own needs far above your instruction.

Lord (or Goddess, Universe, Angels, Spirit, Ascended Masters, Protectors, etc.), I am now asking for restoration. Please restore my health; peace of mind; fruitfulness; property and breakthrough. Restore to me whatever has been tampered with in my life as a result of the witchcraft of false visioners and false preachers. I break every bond, tie and spiritual connection between me and demonic entities

I declare a total restoration and healing of any part of my life that has been tampered with by my ignorant submission to the Great Deceiver.

Amen and Blessed Be.

Prayers and Spells to Destroy Curses and Spells

#1 - Prayer designed to destroy self-inflicted curses

This is the prayer which I used to break my own self-inflicted curse. Although it is rather rare to accidentally curse one's self, it is common enough for there to be a recommended prayer! Remember, the tip of the day is: Research any "names" you are unfamiliar with before throwing them around! Just in my personal experience, I repeated this exact prayer every day for 10 days before I felt the relief from this curse.

Heavenly Father (or Goddess, Universe, Angels, Spirit, Ascended Masters, Protectors, etc.), You have said that the power of death and life is in the tongue; and that we will be justified or condemned by our words. Lord (or Goddess, Universe, Angels, Spirit, Ascended Masters, Protectors, etc.), I know that Your words are ever true. Heaven and earth will pass away, but Your words will not.

Lord (or Goddess, Universe, Angels, Spirit, Ascended Masters, Protectors, etc.), I acknowledge that I have used my words in ways that were not decent and pleasing to You. I have used my words to hurt others, speak negative things about my life, partner, children, family, and nation. I now ask You to forgive all my wrong use of words from the past to present.

Sanctify my tongue and purify my heart. Empower me to be a carrier and speaker of life, health, encouragement, and peace from today onwards.

Whatever pain and hurt I have brought upon myself, my family, my career, my children, and my family as a result of my wrong use of words in the past, heal and restore me today.

I decree that no corrupt word will proceed out of my mouth again. I willingly command myself to put away all forms of bitterness, wrath, anger, malice and evil speaking from today. I command myself to be kind to others, tenderhearted, forgiving, and ever ready to be a blessing.

I break any curse I have imposed upon myself ignorantly, through my use of negative words, anger, fear and anxiety. I replace all self-inflicted pains and events in my life today with God's (or Goddess', Universe's, Angels', Spirit's, Ascended Masters', Protectors', etc.) favor, peace and deliverance.

I bless myself from now onwards; I bless my home; I bless my career; I bless my family; and I bless my children. When and where others are saying there is a casting down, I will be there to ensure there is a lifting up.

Amen and Blessed Be.

#2 - Prayer designed to destroy curses placed on parents

Today, Lord (or Goddess, Universe, Angels, Spirit, Ascended Masters, Protectors, etc.), I thank You for my parents and guardians. I thank You for giving them the grace to bring me into this world. I thank You for enabling them to care for and protect me and my siblings over the years.

I ask forgiveness for my actions which in any way dishonored or disrespected my parents or guardians in the past. I was ignorant. Please have mercy upon me now.

I pray today that You heal and restore my relationship with my parents and guardians. Give me the grace to forgive them if, in any way, I feel they have not treated me right in the past. As I take new steps to make amends with them, may Your power prevail in our hearts and may Your peace and love be established in our hearts once more.

From this day forward, I declare a break to every curse, negative word and evil pronouncement from my parents or guardians in the past. I receive deliverance from the consequences of these statements from today. And I decree healing and restoration from every hurt and pain affecting our lives as a result of these past statements.

Today, I exercise myself into forgiveness and willfully forgive my children, grandchildren, and anyone whom I cared for in the past that offended me. I drop all burdens against every one of them and release everyone from whatever curse is happening in their lives as a result of this harbored pain in my heart.

Amen and Blessed Be.

#3 - Prayer to break a multi-generational curse

Lord (or Goddess, Universe, Angels, Spirit, Ascended Masters, Protectors, etc.), I call upon you to give thanks for all of the blessings you have bestowed upon me. Your light, your love and your power has given me comfort and refuge throughout my life.

I rely on your promises Lord (or Goddess, Universe, Angels, Spirit, Ascended Masters, Protectors, etc.) now as I ask for relief. An ancestor has broken their relationship with you or gone against your demand or has been attacked by evil which follows me through the blood. I beseech you relieve me of this curse; this evil which has plagued those of my blood for untold generations.

You are my protector and my strength and I will follow you all the days of my life.

Amen and Blessed Be.

#4 - Spell to break a multi-generational curse

What you will need:

- A small bag or locket-style necklace

- Sea or Mineral Salt

- Coriander (Cilantro)

- A small drop of your blood (to be harvested during ritual)

- A black candle

- A Selenite crystal

Instructions:

It is an extremely important portion of this spell work that you be as cleansed as possible prior to performing this ritual. You should bathe in saltwater, cleanse your energetic aura with incense, focus your intention, and calm your mind.

This spell should be performed on the night of a full moon.

First, cast your protective circle. Light the black candle. Use the flame to calm your spirit and set your intention - you will be undoing powerful dark magic that is transferred through generations. When you feel focused, place a small amount (a pinch) of the sea salt into the bag or locket. Harvest the small drop of blood and put the blood onto the salt. Next, add the coriander (cilantro). Take up the Selenite crystal. Slowly moving the crystal above the bag or locket, recite the following:

"A darkness has followed

in the blood of rich and poor.

I purify with salt and fire

to be accursed nevermore."

Next, add one drop of wax from the candle. Tie the bag closed or close the locket. Keep this bag or necklace on your person every day until the next full moon. At that time, you may decide whether to dispose of the bag/locket or to keep it.

It is most assuredly odd to include blood into a white magick spell. The reason blood is included in this spell is due to the type of curse (multi-generational). The power of the curse and the negativity is transferred and travels through the bloodline from generation to generation. Therefore, the only way to break the curse is to cleanse the blood of the curse. That is done through the purifying salt and the Selenite crystal. The cilantro is meant to contain the curse within the bag. There are times when the necessity of using bodily fluids in white magick does come up, but as you read other spell books or Books of

Shadows, be aware that most uses of blood or bodily fluids are linked to the dark uses of black magick.

#5 - Prayer to break a curse and reverse the evil

I call upon the power of the earth; the power of the air; the power of the fire; and the power of the water. I call upon the power of the high God and Goddess (or Lord, Universe, Angels, Spirit, Ascended Masters, Protectors, etc.). I call upon the power of the sun and of the moon.

An evil has been levied against me from the realm of darkness; a magick of torment and pain. I hereby break the power of this witchcraft and rebuke the Caster of Darkness. No form of evil or torment shall be given foothold within my life, the life of my family, nor my current or future objective holdings.

In light and love

I implore of thee

Return this evil

With the Rule of Three.

Amen and Blessed Be.

#6 - Prayer to break a curse and reverse the evil

Dear Lord (or Goddess, Universe, Angels, Spirit, Ascended Masters, Protectors, etc.), you have told us, your faithful, that your protection is infinite and that your love is boundless. You have never given us any indication that you will ever let us down, that you will ever turn your back on us. I call upon you now at a time in need. Lord (or Goddess,

Universe, Angels, Spirit, Ascended Masters, Protectors, etc.), I ask that you step between my soul and the curse which has been placed as my personal burden. Whether this curse has been placed on me, my family or my property, I ask that you remove this darkness now. Shine your light and love upon the darkness which has been placed upon me and send it running.

Lord (or Goddess, Universe, Angels, Spirit, Ascended Masters, Protectors, etc.), as in your teachings that one should not suffer a witch to live, I ask that you send the darkness placed on me back to the witch whom birthed this abomination. This person should be forced to feel the negativity and evil which has been unleashed upon your child. Protect me oh Lord (or Goddess, Universe, Angels, Spirit, Ascended Masters, Protectors, etc.) and free me from this curse.

Amen and Blessed Be.

#7 - Spell to break a curse and reverse the evil

You Will Need:

- A mirror

- A piece of paper

- A black pen

- A white candle

- A piece of white fabric

Instructions:

Sometimes just breaking a curse is not enough and doesn't give you closure on the attack. Instead, we aim to break the curse and send the negativity back to the cursing witch.

Cast a protective circle. Light the white candle. Lay the mirror on the altar, reflection side up. Next, on the piece of paper, write all of the symptoms you are experiencing from the curse. Then, lay the paper upside down on the mirror and cover it all with the fabric. Recite the following:

"Your magick delivered

A curse unto me.

I remove and return

Your curse back to thee."

Press on the mirror through the fabric until it breaks (or smash it with a tool).

Gather all of the pieces for disposal. Be careful not to either cut yourself on the shards, or see your reflection in any of the shards.

Close the protective circle.

#8 - Prayer to break a curse

Lord (or Goddess, Universe, Angels, Spirit, Ascended Masters, Protectors, etc.), it is written that they shall gather together, but their gathering is not of You. Whoever gathers against me shall scatter and fall.

I, therefore, command this day, let a furious east wind from heaven confuse, scatter and paralyze every evil gathering against my life and my family.

Amen and Blessed Be.

#9 - Prayer to break a curse

I come to you on my knees Lord (or Goddess, Universe, Angels, Spirit, Ascended Masters, Protectors, etc.). Having prostrated myself before you I ask that you fulfill your promise to your people, that no evil shall assail us if we are with you. Lord (or Goddess, Universe, Angels, Spirit, Ascended Masters, Protectors, etc.), I am under attack from the powers of darkness. Break this attack. With a snap of your mighty fingers, you have the power to undo all that has assailed me.

My life is your Lord (or Goddess, Universe, Angels, Spirit, Ascended Masters, Protectors, etc.). I am assured by your word that you will free me from these bonds of evil.

Amen and Blessed Be.

#10 - Prayer to break a curse of judgment

I decree this night, let every satanic altar and court existing against my life and family, raising accusations and counter-accusations against me and my destiny, be destroyed.

Every demonic lawyer and judge giving judgments against my life, family and destiny, in the spirit wherever you are, I command you all to die by fire.

I nullify every evil judgment and decision that has been made and is being carried out against my life and family. I command all those carrying out such judgments against my family and me to become frustrated.

Let the imagination of every satanic monitor fail and tumble into the abyss. Let every witchcraft mirror monitoring my star break and scatter.

Amen and Blessed Be.

#11 - Prayer to break curse

Lord (or Goddess, Universe, Angels, Spirit, Ascended Masters, Protectors, etc.), I will live to eat the fruit of my labor. Any man or woman, witch or wizard, who has vowed that I will not see good in life, let fire from heaven visit them and destroy their curses.

Amen and Blessed Be.

#12 - Prayer to break curse or negativity

Deliver us Father (or Goddess, Universe, Angels, Spirit, Ascended Masters, Protectors, etc.), from the everyday attacks on our conscious, health, relationships, and beyond. From what we can see coming and from what we would never expect, protect and deliver us from anything that threatens to throw us off your course for our lives. Give us strength to love people that are seemingly unlovable without compromising our character. Build a confidence in us that is unstoppable and immovable, but guard our hearts from pride. Deliver us from our distorted thoughts, sickness, debt, sadness, struggles, hunger, pain, fear, oppression, conflict and unbelief, for we proclaim your peace over our lives through prayer.

Amen and Blessed Be.

#13 - Brute force spell to break curse

You will need:

- Air drying clay

- Water charged with the sun's energy (solar water)

- A slip of paper and pen

- Bay leaf

- Black candle

- Fire-safe container

- Toothpick

Instructions:

Perform spell at night during the new moon.

Cleanse yourself and your protective circle. Anoint yourself with solar water. Light the black candle. Write down on the slip of paper all of the effects that the curse has had on you (be thorough and specific). Fold the paper around the bay leaf. Set the bundle on fire and place it in the fire-safe container.

When the ashes are finished smoldering, set them aside. Take a portion of clay and anoint it with a drop of solar water. Mix the ashes into the clay thoroughly. Roll the clay into a ball and then flatten it into a disk shape. On one side of the disk, use the toothpick to inscribe: "No more befouled, again unbound, again unbidden". On the other side of the disk, inscribe a symbol to represent the curse (it can either be a sigil or just a simple doodle that represents the curse to YOU). Close your protective circle, blow out the candle and allow the talisman to dry

.

Once the talisman is dry, take it outside and allow it to sit and charge in the sun. Carry the talisman with you constantly to allow it to absorb the energy from the curse. On the next new moon, take the talisman and smash it, rendering the curse that the talisman has absorbed broken. Dispose of the shards outside of your home. Be sure that no residue of the talisman remains in your home or on your person.

Prayers and Spell to Destroy Unholy Covenants and Agreements

#1 - Prayer to Destroy Unholy Covenant

God (or Goddess, Universe, Angels, Spirit, Ascended Masters, Protectors, etc.), I come before you to confirm by faith that I stand on and agree with Your word; that I am crucified with Christ; nevertheless I live and that Christ is alive in me. Therefore, God (or Goddess, Universe, Angels, Spirit, Ascended Masters, Protectors, etc.), my testimony is this: Through the blood of Jesus, I am redeemed out of the hand of the devil, in spirit, in body, and in body. Thank you Jesus that your blood speaks for me before God night and day on the mercy seat. Thank you Lord for grace and mercy.

I come before you and I renounce, rebuke, revoke and cancel all unholy covenants and agreements I have ever made in my life and the lives of my ancestors, going all the way back to the first people. I repent, God (or Goddess, Universe, Angels, Spirit, Ascended Masters, Protectors, etc.), for these unholy covenants and agreements in my life and my ancestors lives and I ask for your grace, mercy and forgiveness. Wash away my sins and wash my ancestral bloodline clean.

I decree today that the only covenant I am in from this day forward is only holy covenant and agreement with God (or Goddess, Universe, Angels, Spirit, Ascended Masters, Protectors, etc.). I also decree this over my bloodline.

God (or Goddess, Universe, Angels, Spirit, Ascended Masters, Protectors, etc.) I ask that all records of unholy covenants and agreements be wiped from my record books and the record books of my ancestors in the courts of heaven and remembered no more.

God (or Goddess, Universe, Angels, Spirit, Ascended Masters, Protectors, etc.) I also ask that me and my bloodline be released and set free from all consequences of these sins. I ask that the new holy covenant that I have with you God (or Goddess, Universe, Angels, Spirit, Ascended Masters, Protectors, etc.) be written and decreed in my record books in heaven.

Amen and Blessed Be.

#2 - Prayer for Release from Unholy Covenants and Agreements

Lord (or Goddess, Universe, Angels, Spirit, Ascended Masters, Protectors, etc.), I ask You for grace and strength to obey Your word henceforth. Help me by the Spirit and keep me in constant reminder that I do not have to make promises and pledges to please men, but to obey You.

As I begin to work towards fulfilling my pledges from today, grant me wisdom and speedy breakthrough from this day forward.

Amen and Blessed Be.

#3 - Prayer for Release from Unholy Covenants and Agreements

God (or Goddess, Universe, Angels, Spirit, Ascended Masters, Protectors, etc.), through your forgiveness and your grace, I come humbly before you requesting that you grant me release from my unholy covenant. Lord (or Goddess, Universe, Angels, Spirit, Ascended Masters, Protectors, etc.), I made this covenant in error, against your wishes. Please forgive me for not trusting you to provide all that I may need. I ask that you free me from the bonds of the covenant so that I may devote myself, in body, soul and mind, to your praise.

Amen and Blessed Be.

#4 - Spell for Release from Unholy Covenant

You will need:

- Mugwort

- Salt

- Red Candle

- Small Bowl

Instructions:

Cast your protective circle. Light the red candle.

Add a small amount of crushed Mugwort to the small bowl while reciting, "With herb I signify the power of my word."

Add a small amount of salt to the small bowl while reciting "With salt I signify the purity of my word."

Drip the liquid candle wax into the small bowl while reciting "With wax I signify the binding of my word."

Once the wax has hardened, it should contain bits of the salt and Mugwort.

Take the disk of wax into both hands. Holding it outside of the bowl, break or tear the disk while reciting "Through freedom sought. Through freedom found. My word revoked. No longer bound. So mote it be."

Keep the two parts of the wax from touching each other and bury them outside of your home separate from each other.

#5 - Prayer for Release from Unholy Agreement

I come before you Lord (or Goddess, Universe, Angels, Spirit, Ascended Masters, Protectors, etc.) and confess my foolishness. Your word says that those who do not fulfill their vows and pledges are fools and that You do not delight in them.

How foolish have I been all this while!

Lord (or Goddess, Universe, Angels, Spirit, Ascended Masters, Protectors, etc.) I sincerely apologize for saying things and making commitments that I could not keep afterwards. Please forgive me and set me free from the restrictions from this attitude.

Amen and Blessed Be.

#6 - Prayer for Release from Unholy Agreement

With my mouth, I confess that I am seated with God (or Goddess, Universe, Angels, Spirit, Ascended Masters, Protectors, etc.) in the heavenly places, far above all principalities and powers. I have been translated from the kingdom of darkness in the kingdom of light. I am a bringer of light and a salter of lives and destinies. I am moving from glory to glory even now and forever.

Amen and Blessed Be.

Prayers and Spells for Deliverance from Destructive Habits

#1 - Prayer for Deliverance from Destructive Habits

Every bad habit in my life causing a barrier between me and the power of God (or Goddess, Universe, Angels, Spirit, Ascended Masters, Protectors, etc.), let your fire destroy them this moment.

From today, Lord (or Goddess, Universe, Angels, Spirit, Ascended Masters, Protectors, etc.), plant in me an everlasting hatred for every work of the flesh as revealed in your word. I claim my freedom from every destructive habit.

I declare that I am forever free from all spirits of anger, lust, dishonesty, lying, spiritual laziness, pride, exaggeration, alcoholism, smoking, gossiping, and criticizing.

I command you all to leave my life now and return to the abyss.

Amen and Blessed Be.

#2 - Prayer for Deliverance from Destructive Habits

Lord (or Goddess, Universe, Angels, Spirit, Ascended Masters, Protectors, etc.), whatever evil effect is happening in my life, resulting from my character, past mistakes, or addictions to negative thoughts, words and actions, please set free.

Whatever curse and obstacle my wrong association and friendships have brought upon my life, Lord (or Goddess, Universe, Angels, Spirit, Ascended Masters, Protectors, etc.), let them be destroyed today.

From now onwards, surround me with the right people; surround me with people who will challenge me towards a Godly and excellent life.

I commit myself never to walk in the counsel of the unholy, nor stand in the way of sinners.

Cause me by your Spirit to find delight in seeking You and following holy counsel. Make me like a tree planted by the riverside that will bear fruit in all seasons.

Amen and Blessed Be.

#3 - Spell for Deliverance from Destructive Habits

You Will Need:

- A small box with a lid

- 1 clove of garlic

- 1 sprig of rosemary

- A handful of graveyard dirt

- A symbol of the destructive habit (needs to symbolize it to you)

- A roll of pennies

- Shovel

Instructions:

During a full moon, leave the box you have chosen outside to allow the moonlight to charge the box.

Over the following two weeks, whenever you think about the destructive habit, place one of the pennies into the box. At first, you may go through A LOT of pennies, but it will start to lessen as the days go on.

On the first night of the waning moon, add the rosemary and garlic to the box. Take the symbol of the destructive habit into your hands. Tell the symbol that you "Will not allow this to have any effect in your life ever again." Place the symbol into the box. Secure the lid onto the box with glue or nails.

Take the box and the small amount of graveyard dirt to a location off of your property, but near a moving body of water. Dig a small hole and place the box inside. Sprinkle the box with the graveyard dirt and then bury the box with the rest of the soil. When finished, walk away and do not look back.

Prayers and Spells for Protection

#1 - Incantation for Protection of Body and Spirit

This quick incantation and visualization let you protect yourself when an unexpected threat appears.

Recite the following incantation (even if under your breath):

"Power of the Goddess (or Goddess, Universe, Angels, Spirit,

Ascended Masters, Protectors, etc.).

Power of the God (or Goddess, Universe, Angels, Spirit,

Ascended Masters, Protectors, etc.).

Cool as a breeze.

Warm as a stove.

Flowing like a stream.

Solid as a stone.

So mote it be!"

Repeat the incantation a total of seven times. During each incantation, visualize an electric blue ring of flame encircling you until you have a seven-ring spiral from head to toe.

#2 - Spell for Spiritual and Mental Protection

You will need:

- A golden candle

- A pair of earplugs

- A flat stone, or a piece of wood, or a piece of metal (as amulet)

- Gold paint and a brush

Instructions:

Cast a protective circle. Light the candle and say, "This is the power of silence." Put in the earplugs. Concentrate on the power of spiritual and mental stillness as is found in the candle flame. When you feel calm and still, paint the bindrune on the amulet. Feel the power of the silent stillness flowing from the candle, through you, and into the amulet. Close the protective circle.

Wear or carry the amulet whenever you feel the need for spiritual and mental protection. The amulet can be recharged from time to time by using a new golden candle.

#3 - Prayer for Spiritual and Mental Protection from Evil

Dear Lord (or Goddess, Universe, Angels, Spirit, Ascended Masters, Protectors, etc.), lead me not into temptation, but deliver me from the Evil One. Open my eyes to see the temptations and evil in this world for what they are. Give me a discerning heart, eyes that can see clearly, and ears that can hear you. Help me to resist the lure of temptations that lead me from you and keep my life firmly rooted in light. Protect my loved ones from temptation and evil, surround them with your hedge of protection Lord (or Goddess, Universe, Angels, Spirit, Ascended Masters, Protectors, etc.). Help us to suit up in your armor to withstand the forces of evil in this world. Lead us away from temptation and protect us from the evil in this world.

Amen and Blessed Be.

#4 - Prayer for Protection from Evil

Our loving Heavenly Father (or Goddess, Universe, Angels, Spirit, Ascended Masters, Protectors, etc.), I pray that you protect my family and me from all the evil, as well as from those who would seek to harm us. Guard us and protect us from all the evil which surrounds our lives. Give us your shield of safety and security and place guards at our home door. Lord (or Goddess, Universe, Angels, Spirit, Ascended Masters, Protectors, etc.), please keep our hearts fearless and fill us with your peace, which surpasses all of our understanding.

Thank you for being our refuge and strength. You are the omnipresent help in difficult times. In your faithfulness, we will not be afraid of all the world's dangers. Stay with us wherever we go and keep us in your loving hands.

Amen and Blessed Be.

#5 - Prayer for Protection from Evil Enemies

God (or Goddess, Universe, Angels, Spirit, Ascended Masters, Protectors, etc.), hear my voice and my prayer. I pray that you save me from my enemies and their evil ways. Help me to recognize their bad intentions. Do not let the false and hurting words of them touch me. Protect from devastating enemies' actions. Please do not let evil destroy and triumph over my life. God (or Goddess, Universe, Angels, Spirit, Ascended Masters, Protectors, etc.), I can rely only on you this bad hour and only you can save and protect me. I believe and trust you and you alone.

Amen and Blessed Be.

#6 - Prayer for Protection from Evil - The Lord's Prayer

Our Father who art in Heaven, hallowed be thy name. Thy kingdom come, thy will be done on Earth as it is in Heaven. Give us this day our daily bread and forgive us our trespasses, as we forgive those who trespass against us. Lead us not into temptation, but deliver us from evil. For thine is the kingdom, the power and the glory forever and ever.

Amen.

#7 - Spell for Protection from Evil Enemies

You will need:

- A piece of paper

- A black pen

- A piece of black string

- A small amount of water

- A freezer (if not performed in sub-freezing outside temps)

Instructions:

On the piece of paper, write the name of the person(s) affecting you. Tie a single knot in the middle of the string. While tying the knot, focus on the negative effects this individual has been causing in your life.

Fold the paper up with the piece of string tucked into the middle. Moisten the paper (you do not want to soak it and obliterate the name or names). Place the paper in the freezer (or in a protected spot outside if performing the spell in sub-freezing temperatures) and leave it there until the situation has passed and the individual is no longer affecting your life negatively.

#8 - Protection of Home

The Witch's Bottle - Witch bottles have been used for at least 400 years to protect the home by creating a magickal double of yourself. The supplies needed are a bit odd, but this is ancient magick after all.

You will need:

- A bottle with a tight cork or cap

- Nails and pins (preferably bent)

- Broken glass pieces and/or broken mirror pieces

- Pieces of string, knotted multiple times

- Your own nail, hair clippings, and bodily fluids (i.e., urine)

- A red or black candle (just to seal the bottle cap)

Instructions:

Put all solid materials into the bottle while reciting "Harm be bound away from me". Add the liquid. Close the bottle and seal with the wax.

Bury the bottle upside down outside the front door of the home, or under the floorboards, or hidden in a remote corner of the lowest point of your home.

The idea behind a Witch's Bottle is that the evil spirits are drawn to the bottle instead of you, and then get trapped by the nails, pins, and knotted string and confused by the broken glass/mirror (like a funhouse mirror maze).

#9 - Protection Spell for Friends and Family

You will need:

- Salt

- Rosemary

- Angelica

- White Dandelion Fluff

- Small Crystal of Either Blue Lace Agate, Carnelian, or Garnet

- Slip of Paper with The Name Of The Person To Protect

- White Sachet or Small White Bag

Instructions:

Place the salt, rosemary, angelica, dandelion fluff, crystal, and the slip of paper into the sachet/bag.

Focus on a visualization of the person. Speak the words, "I send you protection from all that may harm you. I send you the wish of safety. I send you the energies to keep you out of harm's way."

Tie your sachet/bag shut and gently kiss it focusing on your desires to send your friend or family member protection.

Place the sachet/bag in a slightly open window to help send the energies to the friend or family member.

Leave the sachet/bag untouched for a minimum of one hour. Following removal from the window, the sachet/bag can be emptied and cleaned for future use.

#10 - Protection Spell for Traveling

Car Mojo Bag - A car mojo bag is a simple but effective way to protect yourself, your passengers, and your vehicle while you are driving. It is also used in a number of other traveling protection spells. I have mine hanging from my rearview mirror, but the car mojo bag can be kept anywhere inside the vehicle. If you do keep it hidden away, be sure to periodically place it on your dashboard at night so it can recharge with moonlight.

You Will Need:

- A small cloth bag (red for machine reliability; orange for travel; or dark blue for luck and long-distance travel)

- A silver paint marker

- A small cup of saltwater

- Choose from the following ingredients, keeping an eye toward balancing elements and properties :

- Fire: An iron nail (protection; dill (protection); cumin seeds (anti-theft)

- Earth: Coffee (alertness); barley (protection); dried corn (protection); malachite (traveler's protection)

- Water: Marjoram (protection); aloe (protection); willow wood (protection); moonstone (traveler's protection)

- Air: Parsley (protection); anise (protection); mint (travel)

Instructions:

The car mojo bag should be created during the waxing moon.

Using the silver paint marker, draw a crescent moon on each side of the cloth bag.

Cast a circle of protection.

Place each ingredient in the bag. As you place each item, announce its purpose. (i.e., "You are for protection.")

Consecrate the bag by sprinkling it with saltwater while reciting:

"Safety from harm. I am protected.

Safety from theft. I am protected.

Safety from attack. I am protected.

Safety from error. I am protected.

Safety from accidents. I am protected.

Safety from hate. I am protected.

Safety from losing my way. I am protected."

Going to each cardinal quarter direction, hold your mojo bag high and recite: "Safety from dangers from the East/South/West/North. I am protected."

Close the protective circle.

#11 - Spell to Protect Against A Dangerous Driver

Road rage is not good for anyone. We are all flying around each other in these mechanical death traps as fast as we can. But when one of the drivers on the road begins to make it blatantly clear that they are in no way interested in maintaining the social contract we all have to drive carefully, they become a threat to everyone else on the road. Something should be done to protect ourselves from harm.

You will need:

- Your car mojo bag

- To keep both eyes on the road!

Instructions:

Hold your car mojo bag in one hand.

Take a deep breath; focus your energy while keeping your eyes on the road.

Visualize the deity of justice of your choice. Personally, I visualize Athena, Goddess of Justice. Athena carries a helmet, spear, a shield, and sometimes an owl with her.

As you exhale, let go of the mojo bag, point at the dangerous driver, and demand justice by literally speaking, "Justice!".

#12 - Prayer for Protection Throughout Long Distance Car Travel

Father (or Goddess, Universe, Angels, Spirit, Ascended Masters, Protectors, etc.), I pray that you will guide and protect me (us, my husband, etc.) as I travel a long distance today. Please send your protection to guard me through every turn and every stop. I know that you are able and that you will do all which is in your will.

I believe that you have heard my prayer Lord (or Goddess, Universe, Angels, Spirit, Ascended Masters, Protectors, etc.) and that you will grant me protection all the way until I arrive safely at my destination.

Thank you for being a loving and protective God (or Goddess, Universe, Angels, Spirit, Ascended Masters, Protectors, etc.).

Amen and Blessed Be.

#13 - Prayer for Protection During Airplane Travel

Dear Lord (or Goddess, Universe, Angels, Spirit, Ascended Masters, Protectors, etc.), I pray over the trip we are about to take on this airplane. I pray that no mechanical errors or emergencies will occur. I pray for our pilot, that he or she will be alert, have sharp eyes, and steady hands throughout this flight. I pray for our flight attendants that they will be friendly, alert and adequately prepared for the trip. I also pray for my fellow passengers, that everyone will be in good spirits and in good health. I pray that everyone will make it to their destination safely and under your protection.

Amen and Blessed Be.

Chapter 3

CLEANSING RITUALS & MAINTAINING VICTORY

Performing cleansing rituals is a vital task in sweeping away the last remaining bits of negativity and darkness that may remain after breaking a curse or any type of psychic attack. Picture it this way, you had been shackled to darkness, chained to evil. When you break or explode from a chain, there are tiny bits or shards of metal that go flying off. They may be too tiny to see with your eyes, but if you walk around in bare feet you are guaranteed to end up with a sliver. Breaking a curse, negative soul tie, evil covenant, or agreement tends to leave behind tiny shards of that negativity and evil. If you allow it to remain in your space, your soul is guaranteed to end up with a sliver. When you get free - stay free.

There are many thought processes and beliefs surrounding cleansing rituals. Every religion from Catholic to Hindu to Rosicrucian has its "own". However, the truth is that, when viewed as a whole, they share more similarities than differences. As a result, there is really no harm to be done by trying one, two, or even all of the ritual examples which follow. All are designed to do the same thing: rid the space (and thus the people within the space) of negative energy and ward against the re-emergence of evil. So explore. Find what works best for you, your space, and your lifestyle.

Unlike the majority of tasks in the spiritual realm, a successful cleansing will result in immediate relief. Oftentimes, although not always, when there is a negative presence or evil remnants are left from the breaking of a curse or spell, a general feeling of heaviness or unease will pervade a space. The stronger the negativity, the stronger the feeling. When you are able to rid your space of the negativity, the feeling of unease, and the heavy atmosphere will disappear along with it. You will know that it worked because you will feel that it worked.

It is extremely important to continue cleansing until all the evil and negativity have been removed. An evil or negative entity can be further enraged and empowered by a half-hearted attempt at cleansing it. The cleansing rituals quite literally hurt and weaken the entity. If the cleansing is not carried through, the entity will resume its prior actions with much greater resolve and a newfound revenge-filled rage. Remember, we are making things better, not worse.

Cleansing Rituals

1. Smudging

Smudging is probably the most widely accepted and practiced cleansing ritual. Smudging is the burning and smoldering of herbs wherein the smoke is used as the cleansing agent. The most commonly used herb for smudging is a bundle of sage, specifically white sage. Sage is the kryptonite of dark entities (whether they be demons or restless spirits). However, a variety of different herbs have actually proven equally effective, including basil, lavender, and clove.

The "ritual" is actually extremely simple. It is one of the few rituals to preferably be performed during the daylight hours.

A smudging session should begin with a prayer or call for protection for anyone who will be in the home during the session. Next, the aura and body of each person present for the session should be cleansed. This is done by lighting the herb bundle and, once it is smoldering, tracing the outline of the person with the bundle; allowing the smoke to rid the aura and individual of any attachments they may be carrying.

Be sure to have at least one window or door open on each floor of the home. The negativity must be given a way to escape or it will be trapped and further enflamed.

Next, the smudging bundle should be carried into each corner of each room and public space in the home. Carry something to catch any of the smudge bundle ashes that may drop off (I use an abalone shell). Do not forget closets, basements, attics, side rooms, enclosed porches, etc. Once each and every space has been cleansed, you have finished the ritual.

There really are not any specific words that must be said during a smudging session. It is really up to those present to use visualization to help the smoke guide the negativity out of the home. However, some tend to give a short prayer or incantation within each room. If you choose to speak, commit to it being in each space and keep it simple.

Perhaps something like, "In the name of the Father, the Son, and The Holy Spirit, I implore all negativity and evil to leave this space. You have no right here." or "Through the power of the Spirit, no negativity or evil shall remain in this home."

Smudging is not even a ritual that should be used only to cleanse from a brush with evil. I smudge myself and my aura once every two weeks and my home 3-4 times per year. It is a great way to maintain a clean aura and stay free of unguided attachments by evil entities and to keep my home clear of pockets of negativity. (Speaking of pockets of negativity - I have two teenagers, so when I finish smudging my home, I always run upstairs and "make sure they are both still there". That gets an eye roll EVERY time! Sometimes, a sense of humor is a witch's best friend.)

2. Salting

Salting is a widespread practice in eastern cultures, but it is quickly becoming accepted by the west as well. Salt has long been known as a purifier. Like quartz, salt's crystalline structure has the ability to hold and trap negative energies. It is a passive way of cleansing your environment of darkness

There are a few different ways of deploying salt as a cleansing agent.

A bowl of salt beside the front door (perhaps on a foyer table) can be used to attract and trap negativity or evil from individuals entering your home.

Salt can be sprinkled in the corners of rooms in order to draw the negativity. Be sure not to touch the salt while it is deployed as a cleanser. After 4-5 days, vacuum or sweep up the salt and dispose of it.

Salt can be used to encircle the outside of a home as a protective measure against the invasion of evil.

Lastly, salt can be added to bathwater to create a cleansing soak for the individual working with the spirit realm.

It is important to note that I am not referring to common table salt. Table salt has been processed with iodine. Iodine affects the structure and clarity of the salt crystals. You will want to use whole or shaved pieces of unrefined sea salt or unrefined mineral salt. Don't worry, it is not as difficult to find as it sounds! A simple Google search will bring up many inexpensive suppliers.

3. Incense

The use of incense began, as far as we can tell, with the Egyptians who used it in healing rituals and the Babylonians who relied upon it when conferring with their divine oracles. The use of incense arrived in Japan in the sixth century - where it was used in purification rituals for the emperor and his court.

Today, incense can be found in a large number of scents and forms. Not to mention incense holders ranging from simple to amazingly intricate.

Incense is best used for personal and small area cleansing. Much like smudging, the smoke is the cleansing agent. However, unlike smudging, incense remains situated in one room.

Just light the tip, blow out the flame and place the incense in the holder.

4. Tuning Fork

Sound and music have been used in healing rituals for thousands of years. Early civilizations used singing bowls for sound therapy and Greek physicians used instruments and vibration to treat sickness and combat insomnia. Using a tuning fork for cleansing is merely an extension of the same idea. Tuning forks vibrate at specific frequencies. The frequency of 417 Hz is known as a "Solfeggio frequency" and has been found to rid the body, mind, and physical space of negative energy. It is not an absolute "must", but a fork tuned to the frequency of 417 Hz would undoubtedly be the most useful.

Find a comfortable spot within each room of your home. Set your intention for a cleared, renewed space. Lightly tap the tuning fork against something solid. Close your eyes and let the sound vibrate around and through you; allow it to clean all of the negativity and evil out of the room and you. Move on to the next room and repeat the process.

What cleansing is NOT?

I felt that this point was important enough that it required its own section. Blessing a house and home exorcism is NOT what is meant by "cleansing". Let me be very clear because I do want to allow room for any ambiguity on this point: Do not, under any circumstances, attempt to perform your own "Home Blessing" or "Home Exorcism". A blessing or exorcism should only ever be performed by an experienced priest, clergy member, or shaman.

Let's discuss why. The most dangerous work you could possibly undertake is attempting to remove a demon from your space. And remember, you do not need to believe in demons because they certainly believe in you. If goodness exists, it must have a counterpart. If goodness exists, evil must exist as well. Therefore, we are going to simply assume that you believe in the concept and reality of demonic forces.

The cleansing tactics explained previously are useful and safe for removing the shards, the pieces, and remnants of evil left behind after a psychic attack is broken. They are not, however, designed to remove a full evil presence - a demon - or even a fully negative soul.

An attempt by an individual who is not appropriately protected, shielded, and fully prepared to bless or exorcise a home or space can easily result in very unwanted effects. These types of half-hearted attempts have led to a sharp increase in the intensity of the evil attack, the opening of a portal allowing other evil entities to gain access to the space, personal evil attachment, or even full possession of the living by a demonic entity.

It is not just ill-advised, it is not just probably something you should be careful of, and it is not a good way to show off for friends and flex your spiritual muscles. It is something you should completely rule out right now and steer clear of. The very last thing that I would want to occur is for one of you, my friends, my family, or anyone to ever be hurt as a result of not understanding the dangers of blessing a home or attempting to exorcise a home. Be smart. Stay safe.

Symbols, Stones, and Protective Objects

There are a handful of symbols, stones, and protective objects that you may want to be aware of and/or have on hand if you have been touched by evil. We are not going to get into a fully comprehensive guide to symbology and crystals because that could easily fill two or three other volumes, however we should at least touch on a few of the highlights.

Symbols

We live in a symbolic world. Because symbols hold the power to be immediately recognizable and to mean paragraphs worth of information, they were being used prior to the development of language to transfer information and ideas. We are going to briefly discuss three symbols that can definitely be of use in protecting ourselves from all forms of psychic attack: The Pentacle; The Triquetra; and The Eye of Horus.

- **The Pentacle**

The Pentacle, a five-pointed upright star within a circle, symbolizes white magick; light, goodness, and intellect. It is often used or worn as a talisman.

- **The Triquetra**

The Triquetra, or "Triple Moon", symbolizes the threefold nature of reality - the balance between mind, body, and spirit.

- **The Eye of Horus**

The Eye of Horus (the left eye) is related to the moon. It symbolizes protective powers coming from the deflection of evil forces.

Stones and Crystals

Stones and crystals are nature's magickal gift to us all. Formed in many different ways over unimaginable spans of time and under unfathomable conditions, these amazingly powerful objects wait patiently to be used for their intended purposes. They can be beautiful, smooth and shining with what seems like light from within; they can be rough and bulky, they can be as dark black as any starless night, or glimmer with a rainbow full of colors. No matter what form they take, stones and crystals have earned the respect and recognition they have received throughout the centuries as true magickal miracles.

We will only be exploring a few of the thousands of stones and crystals which hold magickal significance because there are thousands of reference books out there dedicated solely to the subject. For our purposes, however, you should have a working knowledge of the following stones and crystals.

- **Black Tourmaline**

Black Tourmaline is a powerful healer and protector crystal. Specifically, it is useful in blocking psychic attacks and negative thought patterns. It is even used as protection against harmful electromagnetic radiation caused by modern electronics.

- **Black Obsidian**

Black Obsidian is formed when molten lava is cooled very quickly, such as when it comes into contact with water. It works wonderfully as a protective shield against negativity and evil. It soaks up bad energy like a sponge and holds it. Because of its retention ability, you will want to cleanse your obsidian regularly by simply holding it under running water and visualizing all of the negativity washing from the stone, down the drain, and out of your life.

- **Selenite**

Selenite has been a favorite among crystal lovers dating back to Ancient Greece. Some Greeks actually made windows from thin slabs of Selenite. It is found deep in the caves of Mexico, Morocco, and Madagascar, and the raw crystal formations in the caves can reach up to 35 feet long. The caves are absolutely beautiful, assuming you would find Superman's Fortress of Solitude to be beautiful! Selenite is very useful in cleansing and clearing a home or office because it dispels negative energy and creates calm in any space. Selenite lamps are also a great alternative to Himalayan salt lamps because it not only looks great when lit but is also self-cleansing and can cleanse other crystals in its environment.

- **Amethyst**

Amethyst has been used since the middle ages as a healing crystal. It is widely used for its ability to protect its bearer emotionally and spiritually by helping to break anxious or addictive thought patterns and ties to stressful energies. Also, a piece of amethyst on your nightstand or under your pillow can help protect you from nightmares.

- **Carnelian**

Carnelian is an absolutely beautiful, polished stone with swirls of red, orange, and brown. It is a great way to stay energized but calm at the same time. It will keep you grounded even when the atmosphere around you is buzzing. Carnelian can make you feel comfortable without the effects of laziness or complacency.

- **Clear Quartz**

Clear quartz is an extremely dynamic and versatile crystal. It is useful in both deflecting negativity and attracting positivity. Also, clear quartz is easily able to pick up and funnel intention. Just as it does in its use in laser functionality, in television projection tubes and in early computer motherboards, clear quartz is a ready-made energy storage and amplification device.

- **Smoky Quartz**

This opaque gray crystal is a personal favorite. Smoky Quartz helps you in manifesting your desires out of the ethereal plane and into the material world. But the beautiful part is that, once you have made your ideas into reality, smoky quartz will also protect those intentions from any evil or negative energies that may attempt to get in the way.

- **Black Jade**

Black jade can help you stay clear of negative people and situations by helping you tune into the root source of the negativity. Sometimes it is just easier to avoid contact with negativity than it is to try to rid yourself of it. Black Jade is also known to assist you in tapping into your intuition.

- **Smithsonite**

Smithsonite is a soothing stone that can help calm your emotions and connect you to your center. Having a calm mind and a grounded center is absolutely vital to the success of many of the spells, rituals, and prayers we have discussed. Plus, who couldn't use some help relaxing after a stressful day or event!

- **Limestone**

Any witch who already practices, or spiritualist familiar with crystals, is undoubtedly confused by this addition. Limestone is not usually included in a list of stones or crystals used in any kind of spell work. However, limestone is very special. Limestone is found as bedrock in non-sandy environments and is often used to build the foundation of many of the homes in these non-sandy environments. And a special quality of this common stone is that it contains natural clear quartz and silica. Within the metaphysics community, limestone is seen as a storage vessel for energy. There is also the paranormal theory that limestone allows for storage and release (playback) of high-energy situations. For these reasons, I always include a piece of limestone with me during a cleansing session and keep one nearby during meditation.

Protective Objects

There are also protective objects that can be helpful in dissuading curses, evil energies, and psychic attacks. We have actually already spoken about three of them: The Witch's Bottle, The Car Mojo Bag, and The Pentacle. There are just a few more objects that I tend to keep on hand in case of a psychic attack. They are Black Salt, Amulets, Talismans, and Candles.

- **Sea Salt or Mineral Salt**

We have already discussed how useful sea salt or mineral salt can be in cleansing you or your space. However, salt is useful in any number of rituals. It is the ultimate purifier. Salt represents purity, goodness, and light. I personally use sea salt when casting my protective circles in order to protect myself from any negativity getting too close to me while working in the spirit realm. I also circle my home with a sea salt line once per month to keep all negativity and evil spirits out of my living space. It is believed that evil is unable to cross a salt line because of its purity, unless carried or attached to a human.

- **Black Salt**

Black Salt is a useful ritualistic tool used in a number of protection spells to keep unwanted energies at arm's length, though not as mystical and mysterious as it sounds. Black Salt is, essentially, just ashy sea or mineral salt. If I find myself low on black salt, I will typically make my own by burning some pinecones to ash. Then I collect the ash and add it to a bag of moistened salt, mix it around, and spread it out to dry in the sun. You can also add complementary herbs to the mixture if the black salt has a specific purpose.

- **Amulets and Talismans**

First of all, the terms "amulet" and "talisman" can and often are used interchangeably. Their definitions, however, do differ. An amulet is an object with natural magickal properties. As such, crystals and stones would be considered amulets. A talisman, on the other hand, is a created object which must be charged with magickal powers by its creator. Talismans are usually created for a specific reason, whereas an amulet would be used for general protection from evil and negativity.

- **Candles**

Individuals who work with the spirit realm have candle collections to rival any Yankee Candle Co. outlet! Candles are used in every practice from casting a protective circle to aromatherapy and everything in between. The color of the candle is very important in spell work as the color itself is used symbolically. The flickering flame can be used for divination or to facilitate a meditative state, as well as obviously for burning paper. Scented candles are rarely used in spell work, however they are extremely useful in aromatherapy applications and for placing a person in the proper state of mind for carrying out their work in the spirit world.

Understanding Blessings and Prosperity

So many times, I have seen people who have successfully broken curses or defended themselves in a psychic attack be afraid to follow through and manifest the blessings and prosperity in their life. They seem to feel like being given the help and blessing of the broken curse is really all they could have hoped for. But there is no such limitation placed on our blessings from the universe or any deity. We should never be hesitant to request our fruits. They are FOR us.

Should we be treating the universe or God or the Goddess, etc. as a lottery ticket? Absolutely not. Let's be honest here, if we could guarantee the next Mega-Millions jackpot by praying hard or by performing the right ritual, there would never be a week without a winner! That is just not how the spiritual plane works. Our blessings and our prosperity do not necessarily mean financial gains. The very concept of money is a human invention and has no value on the astral plane. The blessings and prosperity that await us are much more likely to be in the form of "shalom".

Shalom is a Hebrew term that means peace, completeness, soundness, and welfare. I think of shalom as being comparative to grace. Grace is that which affords joy, pleasure, delight, goodwill, and reward. It is the kindness and benevolence of God (or Goddess, Universe, Angels, Spirit, Ascended Masters, Protectors, etc.).

Manifesting our fruits, our blessings, our prosperity is all about living and walking in the favor afforded us by the universe. There is really nothing more powerful than being in a position of positivity and light wherein we are receiving the blessings meant for us. The curses, the negative soul ties, the covenants, and the agreements we have learned to escape have kept our blessings and prosperity from raining down on us. However, now that we have been freed from the evil weighing us down, the universe is once again in a position to smile upon us.

To manifest and receive the blessings and favors which have awaited us, we need to know how to request them. And for that, we need to discuss some prayers and spells to assist in the manifesting of our fruits. And then we will review some crystals and crystal combinations that can assist you in getting your intention for blessings out into the universe.

Prayers for Manifesting Your Fruits

#1 - Prayer for Manifesting the Fruit of The Spirit

Dear Lord (or Goddess, Universe, Angels, Spirit, Ascended Masters, Protectors, etc.), I desire to remain rooted in you, bearing fruits that lead others to the light of your love.

I desire to walk in love, forgiving others at all times and gifting God's (or Goddess, Universe, Angels, Spirit, Ascended Masters, Protectors, etc.) blessings in my life with others, just as you have done for me.

I desire to walk in joy every day of my life, thereby drawing from the well of salvation.

Please remind and help me at all times to love and be joyful as I live.

Amen and Blessed Be.

#2 - Prayer for Manifesting the Fruit of The Spirit

Dear Lord (or Goddess, Universe, Angels, Spirit, Ascended Masters, Protectors, etc.), I desire to bear the fruit of goodness so that I may lead others to the path you have shown me.

I desire to be faithful at all times with whatever God (or Goddess, Universe, Angels, Spirit, Ascended Masters, Protectors, etc.) blesses me with, so that I may stand before you in the end and receive the rewards of faithfulness.

I desire to be gentle with myself and others, in thoughts, words and actions, so that I may be an instrument of encouragement and uplifting to others and not discouragement.

I desire to walk in self-control in food, dressing and in everything so that I could win the race set before me and not be cast away after teaching others.

I call upon you to empower me every day to bear these fruits as I live, serve God (or Goddess, Universe, Angels, Spirit, Ascended Masters, Protectors, etc.), and relate with others.

Amen and Blessed Be.

#3 - Prayer for Manifesting the Fruit of The Spirit

God, (or Goddess, Universe, Angels, Spirit, Ascended Masters, Protectors, etc.), you are the way and the substance of all life; all that is good, and as your child all that you are is within me.

I now understand my divine birthright and I call it forth letting your everlasting abundance manifest in my life.

You are the source that ignites my dreams and meets my every need in perfect order. I am truly blessed.

Amen and Blessed Be.

#4 - Simple Spell for Manifesting Your Fruits

The first step of this spell should be performed during a new moon.

You will need:

- A slip of paper

- A small box or small bag

- A piece of Clear Quartz, or Citrine, or Amethyst

Instructions:

While holding your crystal, focus your intention on manifesting the fruits of your Spirit (the goodness, the light, the fortune, the luck, the positivity).

On the piece of paper, write what you want to manifest in your life as if you already have it. For instance, if you are attempting to manifest peace in your life, you would write "My life is peaceful. My mind is calm."

Fold the piece of paper and place it, along with the piece of your crystal, into the box or bag. Close the box or bag.

Every day, or every night if more convenient, open the box or bag, remove the paper and the crystal. While holding both, focus your intent again on what you are attempting to manifest. Read what you had written followed by the words, "So mote it be." Place the paper and crystal back into the box or bag. Do this every day or night a minimum of nine times. If you feel that you have not yet seen the manifestation you want, keep reading it daily and focusing on your intent.

Once you see the manifested fruit you desired, burn the paper and spread the ashes outside your home. There is no need to cleanse the crystal or the container. Feel free to use both again immediately if you wish.

Stones and Crystals for General Abundance

- **Aventurine**

Aventurine is known as a crystal of abundance. It can be charged with your intent or combined with other crystals to lend abundance to them.

- **Bloodstone**

This aggressively named stone is actually more like a bank vault than a gusher. Bloodstone will help you in conserving your money. It is perfectly suited for carrying with you on shopping trips, keeping you under control on yard sale days, and for deflecting spells cast to separate you from your wealth.

- **Citrine**

Citrine is known as the Merchant's Stone because it is meant to assist with cash flow. Keep citrine in your wallet, your purse, or above your shop door to see your financial intentions manifest in your life.

- **Jade**

Jade has long been associated with success. It excels in its ability to focus your intent to manifest luck, prosperity, and good fortune.

- **Stibnite**

Stibnite crystals are not exactly a common commodity. However, if you see one of these metallic black crystals for sale, snag it! It is an amazing ability to keep our attention and intentions focused on our manifestation goals. It can also be combined with other crystals to keep us laser-focused. It may not win any beauty contests, but what a powerful crystal!

Combinations for Specific Abundance

- **Aventurine & Rose Quartz**

The combination of Aventurine and Rose Quartz can be used to attract the right people into your love life. These two crystals combine to bring us meaning and fulfillment through the right people or even just that one right person.

- **Pyrite & Amethyst**

The combination of Pyrite and Amethyst is used to bring an abundance of spiritual knowledge and enhanced mindfulness. Because amethyst is the ultimate stone for spiritual advancement, this duo is perfect to accelerate the effects of your meditations, spiritual learning, and path to peace.

- **Emerald & Rhodonite**

This Emerald and Rhodonite combination is perfect to manifest an increase in popularity and an uptick in your social life. And the best part, both of these crystals correspond to forming healthy relationships.

- **Bloodstone & Garnet**

This is your ultimate health and fitness combination. You will find that the combination of Bloodstone and Garnet can provide you with the motivation you need to get fit and healthy.

- **Citrine & Carnelian**

This beautiful combination is something that I refer to as the "Unstoppable Muse". With Citrine for abundance and Carnelian providing its powers of creativity, this duo will fuel your artistic side and provide that inspiration and abundance of ideas all artists need.

Maintaining Your Victory and Deliverance

Once you have broken a curse or spell, destroyed evil soul ties, covenants, and psychic attacks, cleansed yourself and your space of negative energy and evil, and have begun to manifest your fruits, you would think you are done and could just sit back and relax. But no. Just as evil never stops chasing us, we must never stop being vigilant to avoid it.

The next step is maintaining our newfound victory over evil and celebrating our deliverance from its clutches.

Have you ever wondered where the idea arose of demonic entities referring to themselves as being "legion"? Well, it comes from what happens after evil is removed or cleansed from our lives. The Christian Bible describes it this way in the book of Matthew:

> "When the unclean spirit has gone out of a person, it passes through waterless places seeking rest, but finds none.

> Then it says, 'I will return to my house from which I came.' And when it comes, it finds the house empty, swept, and put in order.

> Then it goes and brings with it seven other spirits more evil than itself, and they enter and dwell there, and the last state of that person is worse than the first. So also will it be with this evil generation."

Not exactly inspiring, I know. This passage pretty much boils down to, exorcising an evil demonic entity will lead to being haunted or possessed by that same entity plus seven others that are even worse. Exorcise one of those 8 and you end up with 15 and so on and so on.

You can see how the numbers could quickly get out of hand, especially considering that they are each eviler than their predecessor.

However, this does not need to be the outcome. We are given instructions right in the passage.

First, do not keep your spirit empty. It is important to fill your mind, body, and spirit with positive thoughts and positive vibrations. Work out a system to read or recite positive affirmations every day. It can be just 10 minutes out of your day, but it is part of the process of keeping the evil from gaining an even stronger foothold than before.

Second, exercise your faith by sharing your testimony. You have been victorious! You have defeated evil on a plane that believed you had no chance! Do you need to hide? No! Become active in your faith, whatever faith that is. Be vocal, be joyous, be a beacon of positivity. You have earned the right to be proud of your freedom and the duty to tell others how you achieved it.

Thirdly, keep a positive outlook on life and speak positivity into your life. Now is certainly not the time to allow depression or negativity into any small crack or crevice. Positivity attracts positivity, just as negativity attracts negativity. So, the more positive you are about your future, the more positivity you will create in your future.

But, I believe the most important sentence in this passage is, "And when it comes, it finds the house empty, swept, and put in order." So, when the evil returns to the person, it finds a hospitable and waiting home for it and 7 of its evil brethren. We do not want it to find an acceptable home when evil comes sniffing around us again. We want evil to find us already occupied by God, by light, by spirit. We want to make evil very uncomfortable. That is why we need to maintain our victory and ward ourselves against future attacks.

Once we rid ourselves of an evil, we will ensure that it cannot simply return with backup and take up residence yet again. And we can accomplish this maintenance with prayer.

Prayers to Maintain Victory

#1 - Prayer to Maintain Victory

Heavenly Father (or Goddess, Universe, Angels, Spirit, Ascended Masters, Protectors, etc.), I praise you with all my heart. You are my shield. I take refuge in you all the days of my life and I am safe. Even though the enemy comes like a flood, you have set a standard over my life and I always remain victorious. I call to you Lord (or Goddess, Universe, Angels, Spirit, Ascended Masters, Protectors, etc.), for you are worthy of all praise and I am saved.

Amen and Blessed Be.

#2 - Prayer to Maintain Victory

God (or Goddess, Universe, Angels, Spirit, Ascended Masters, Protectors, etc.), I confess that I have been too concerned with the physical world and have neglected the spiritual. But through victory and deliverance, you have shown me peace and strength. Open the eyes of my heart that I may become all the more aware of the spiritual battles taking place around me. Never allow me to forget that there is a real enemy seeking to destroy me so that I may remain alert and vigilant.

Use the Spirit to awaken me that I may become more attentive, watchful and sober-minded. Grant me wisdom to earlier discern the ways the enemy is attacking me so that I may become more intentional in choosing righteousness.

Amen and Blessed Be.

#3 - Prayer to Maintain Deliverance

Lord (or Goddess, Universe, Angels, Spirit, Ascended Masters, Protectors, etc.), I praise you. This world is hard. It threatens to crush us in many ways. Physically, we cannot always outrun the ailments of our bodies. Sickness and injury take hold of us and we are always healed to the original state of our health. Mentally, we are bombarded and pulled at by unfiltered thoughts threatening to run away with our self-esteem on a daily basis. Spiritually, you promise us a battle in this life. You bring our hearts to focus on your truth at the start of each day, expecting a battle, but also promising deliverance.

Father (or Goddess, Universe, Angels, Spirit, Ascended Masters, Protectors, etc.), in overwhelming moments help us to always recall the truth. Remind us of the great gift you have given us through deliverance; deliverance from all we have battled and fought. Your protective hand of deliverance has guided me into deliverance and light. You are always faithful.

Amen and Blessed Be.

#4 - Prayer to Maintain Deliverance

Heavenly Father (or Goddess, Universe, Angels, Spirit, Ascended Masters, Protectors, etc.), you call us to action, to stand firm in our faith. Help us turn from shame, make a way for kindness, and rise up for those who cannot speak for themselves, and find a way to make sure those who are burdened by distorted thoughts of who they are may experience the deliverance which you have given to me. For you assure us that when we seek you, we will find you if we seek you with all of our hearts.

Father (or Goddess, Universe, Angels, Spirit, Ascended Masters, Protectors, etc.), we are grateful that you hear us and care for us beyond our understanding. We prayerfully proclaim deliverance in our own lives, and in the lives of those suffering next door to us and around the world. We cry out to you in faith that you will continue your promise to deliver us from our physical pain and mental anguish.

Amen and Blessed Be.

Conclusion

Do you feel armed and prepared to do battle in the spirit realm? Do you now feel that you have the tools to protect yourself, your family, and your belongings against psychic attacks through curses, spells, negative soul ties, evil covenants, and agreements? Do you understand the importance and the ways to cleanse yourself, your home, and your surroundings of negativity and evil? I sincerely hope that you do. You have been empowered to break the chains that bind your soul to these evils. You can go on living your life free of the negative entanglements caused by evil, whether you brought it on yourself or it was thrust upon you by other individuals. And you can rest in the assurance that you have the power to prevent the return of evil and destruction from returning. Walk in confidence.

That is what I hope you take with you from this book - the ability to walk in confidence. Although it is strange to say, I honestly hope you never need to use any of the prayers or spells contained here. I would never wish that anyone ever come into contact with negative or evil forces. However, since you have decided that you need to take this journey, your path has most likely already been crossed by evil. The good news is that now you see that you're not powerless to stop the effects. You do not need to simply accept it or try to mitigate the negativity in your life. You, my friends, can remove it.

We all know people who seem to be beaten down by life. Over time, they have come to expect things not to work out for them. They are no longer surprised when plans go awry or they are passed over when something positive happens around them. In my life, I refer to these unfortunate souls as "Eeyores". They just kind of plod through life, content taking the hits and negativity that daily life offers. Willing to feed off the scraps left behind by the energized, forward-looking individuals. It has happened to them so often that it becomes a mindset, a way of life. Well, I say, NO MORE!

In the spirit realm, vibrations cause reality. An example on this plane with which we are all familiar would be sound waves. Sound waves are essentially vibrations in the air caused by the disturbance of silence. These vibrations hit against our eardrums and are interpreted by our brain into meaning. In the world of spirit, vibrations in the stillness caused by our mindful intentions are able to manipulate reality, as if reality were a universe-sized eardrum. The universe then interprets our vibrations and discerns meaning - which changes the reality of our lives.

A little too deep? It boils down to this - How we feel and our focused intent (what is most prevalent in our mind) is the "vibe" we give off. If we give off a positive vibe, we receive positivity in our lives. If we give off a negative vibe, we receive negativity in our lives. Within the ethereal, like always attracts like.

Through the use of the prayers and spells you have learned, you can give off a confident, fearless, positive vibe. You have gained the strongest armor anyone can possibly have against attack - the knowledge of how to be victorious in any style of battle. Not only do you hold the power to repel evil, but you also hold the keys to keeping it away. Forever. Not only have you learned how to wield a sword against evil, but you have also become the sword against evil.

You are familiar with the prayers to invoke the power of God or Goddess, Universe, Angels, Spirit, Ascended Masters, Protectors, etc. into the war for your freedom from oppressive negativity and evil.

You are familiar with the spells to fight fire with fire on the spiritual plane.

You are familiar with the stones and crystals which can focus and amplify your intentions or trap negativity themselves.

You are familiar with the Archangels who you can implore for assistance in a time of crisis.

You are familiar with the symbols from antiquity that can be used to strengthen your defenses against negativity and evil.

You are familiar with the objects you may want to keep on hand to immediately rid yourself of new negative or evil attachments.

You are familiar with the prayers and tactics you should use to maintain your victory over curses, spells, evil soul ties, negative covenants, and agreements.

You are familiar with the tools and tactics necessary to cleanse your aura and your space of negativity or evil.

You have become your own shield and your own sword. Your life is your own to live on your own terms. The universe wants the best for you and your family. The time has come to reclaim your peace and your space. And now, you know exactly what to do.

Message and small request from the Magickal Witches team:

We wish you nothing but magickal success and health on your journey of being a powerful witch! If you've enjoyed this book or found that it has been exactly what you've needed, please consider leaving the book a review here where you can find the book in Glinda Porter's author profile. You will also find all her other literature that you'd love to check out. We're sure of it!

All feedback is extremely important to us because it helps us deliver exactly what you want and it also helps other readers make a decision when deciding on the best books to purchase. We would greatly appreciate it if you could take 60 seconds to leave the book a quick review. You can also reach out via email to leave any feedback.

Email: magick@magickalwitches.com

Website: www.magickalwitches.com

Author Profile: https://www.amazon.com/author/glinda-porter

Lastly, don't forget to claim the "Survival and Wellness Kit for Magickal Witches" by scanning the QR code to receive:

- 10 Elixirs For Detoxification and Aura Cleansing

- 12 Spell Jar Recipes For Protection

- Guide For Talisman Preparation For Use Outside Home

- 20 Daily Detox Tips To Keep Your Vessel Clear

- Master Ingredient Shopping List

Resources

https://thefreedictionary.com

https://witchcraftandwitches.com

Abundance Crystals. Retrieved from https://satincrystals.com/page
s/abundance-crystals

Big Issue North. April 26, 2021

Lipp, Deborah. The Complete Book of Spells - Wiccan Spells For
Healing, Protection, and Celebration. Rockridge Press, 2020.

Moons, M. Spell to Break a Bad Habit (Banish). Retrieved from htt
ps://moodymoons.com/2019/10/31/spell-to-break-a-bad-habit

Mutuku, R. Names of Angels In The Bible and Their Duties. Retrieved from https://yen.com.gh

Okpara, Daniel C. Prayers That Break Curses & Spells & Release Favors & Breakthroughs. Better Life Media, 2016.

Okpara, Daniel C. Prayers To Break Negative and Evil Soul Ties, Agreements and Covenants. Better Life Media, 2016.

Okpara, Daniel C. Prayers To Destroy Witchcraft Attacks & Release Your Blessings. Better Life Media, 2016.

Phillips, G. Something Wiccan This Way Comes-Part 1 of 2. Retrieved from https://musingsfromtheuniverse.com/2021/04/09/something-wiccan-this-way-comes-part-1-of-2

Russell, Jeffrey Burton, and Brooks Alexander. A History of Witchcraft, Sorcerers, Heretics & Pagans. Thames & Hudson, 2007.

Skon, J. Sidestep Negative Energy With These 6 Crystals. Retrieved from https://mindbodygreen.com/2020/02/11/sidestep-negative-energy-with-these-6-crystals

Printed in Great Britain
by Amazon

57440868R00067